22TALK
SHIFTs

TOOLS TO TRANSFORM
LEADERSHIP

IN BUSINESS,
IN PARTNERSHIP
AND IN LIFE

KRISTER UNGERBÖCK

FOUNDER OF THE GLOBAL TALK *SHIFT* MOVEMENT

LIONCREST

PUBLISHING

22 TALK SHIFTS

Tools to Transform Leadership in Business,
in Partnership, and in Life

ISBN   978-1-5445-1480-2 *Hardcover*

          978-1-5445-1479-6 *Paperback*

          978-1-5445-1478-9 *Ebook*

To COVID-19:

If there is any silver lining in the devastation that you've wrought, it is that you ignited The Compassion Revolution in business.

Bon courage,

Krister Ungerböck
Founder of the global TalkSHIFT movement.

Contents

PART 1: THE ESSENTIALS

PART 2: THE LEADER *SHIFTS*
TOOLS TO BUILD BETTER BOSSES—
AND BECOME ONE

PART 3: THE PARTNER *SHIFTS*
TOOLS TO BUILD BETTER PARTNERS—
AND BECOME ONE

PART 1

—

THE ESSENTIALS

The Birth of Talk*SHIFTs*

The beginning of my own communication transformation did not start while I was learning to lead in French and German after establishing the European headquarters of the software company (USI) where I ultimately became CEO. Nor did it start while leading our company from a small team in St. Louis to 3,000 percent growth and hundreds of employees in eight countries worldwide.

I unexpectedly discovered my own need to change how I was communicating, at both work and home, in the most unlikely of places—the YMCA, while signing up for a gym membership.

It was a typical, busy day when I found myself at the YMCA.

A YMCA employee was typing my responses into the computer when she asked the question that changed my life.

"Who is your emergency contact?" she asked.

I paused. And then I broke down crying.

I had no one.

You see, in the weeks leading up to that moment, I had initiated a painful business divorce with my business partner. And at the same time, my wife had decided to divorce me.

My business partner and I had wildly succeeded in business together despite bitter, daily conflict. For 25 years, we argued nearly every time we spoke. He was now 75 years old, and as he got older, the conflict was getting worse. I'd tried coaches, communication experts, psychologists, professional mediators, conflict resolution experts, board members—nothing worked.

By this time, I'd been CEO for nearly five years and, despite the bitter behind-closed-doors conflict, we had managed to double the size of the company.

I concluded that the only way to bring the conflict to an end would be to buy the company. So I challenged him.

"Just name your price. If I can't convince investors to put up enough money to buy you out, then I'm not the right person to be CEO. Consider my offer, and let's find a solution over the coming months," I said.

Less than 24 hours later, without asking a single clarifying question about my offer, he called a short meeting and delivered his response: "There is no price at which I would sell the company to you." And since I had made it clear that I would move on if we couldn't come to an agreement, I resigned.

Twenty-five years earlier, my business partner had dangled the carrot of taking over his business "someday" and lured me away from a dream job in Chicago at one of the most prestigious strategy consulting firms in the world. The allure of becoming CEO upon his retirement spurred me to take a 50 percent pay cut and join him. Within a year, we'd turned around his struggling ten-person business. Within three years, we'd grown 300 percent. Ultimately, we grew the company together into a global software company, winning five consecutive Top Workplaces awards, achieving remarkable employee engagement levels of 99.3 percent, and becoming a dominant player in our niche—event management software.

Our 25-year business partnership ended overnight. To consider my offer, he took less than one hour for every year that I'd worked 60- to 100-hour weeks growing his business.

As I calmly left the meeting, one of my father's favorite phrases echoed in my head: "With friends like that, who needs enemies."

Except my business partner wasn't my enemy.

He was my father.

The Secret Sauce
of Talk*SHIFTs*

Like many business leaders, I was laser-focused on achieving success. I began reading business books as a teenager because I wanted to make my father proud.

Ultimately, it wasn't in business books that I would find the secrets that I was seeking. I went to workshops where I learned the insights that, frankly, I would have dismissed as "touchy-feely" and "woo-woo psychobabble" back in my CEO days.

And it was there that I discovered the secrets that had eluded me all those years as a CEO.

The strikingly simple secret that I learned was this: *little language changes make a big difference*. I finally understood that compassionate communication isn't just a pain to be tolerated only when necessary; it is THE universal secret to leadership that works equally well in business, in relationships, and in life.

A LEADER IN RELATIONSHIPS

As my business relationship with my father ended, my marriage of nine years was ending as well. I became fascinated by the work of Dr. John Gottman, renowned for his research on marriage and divorce. Dr. Gottman is known for his ability to predict divorce with 94 percent accuracy after observing the communication patterns used by couples during an emotionally charged conversation.

While his work was specific to marital relationships, it struck me that the same communication patterns that he used to predict divorce would also have predicted the breakup with my father, as well as every other business "breakup" in my career—executives I'd fired, salespeople who'd left, taking customers to the competition—every one of these "breakups" would have been predicted by Gottman's framework. I began to study the many ways that our communication leads to unintended consequences. What became apparent to me was how often dysfunctional communication patterns are tolerated—sometimes even celebrated—in the workplace.

I asked myself, "What if marriage research could be used to create great working relationships, and business best practices could be used to create great families?"

And this was the inspiration behind the Talk*SHIFTs*.

Now, you may be wondering "Why does the world need a business book to bring families together?"

We often don't invest time to recover relationships until the other person says, "I'm leaving." What the marital research shows is that the person who leaves often decided to leave years before. By the time they say, "I'm leaving," they're already mentally gone. Isn't it often the same with employees? After all, most unhappy employees don't quit and leave, they quit and *stay*. Unfortunately, quitting and staying is quite common in marriages too.

WHAT ARE TALK*SHIFTS*?

Talk*SHIFTs* aim squarely at people who aspire to lead in the broadest sense of the word—those who lead teams, and those who don't; those who lead organizations, and those who aspire to...Talk*SHIFTs* are a collection of simple say-this-not-that rules, fill-in-the-blanks phrases, and powerful questions that can make your day, your year, or your career.

Simply put, Talk*SHIFTs* are tools to build better bosses—and become one—by shifting our words. The Talk*SHIFTs* are a collection of communication **shifts** that impact how we relate to others. A shift is different from a change. Change is slow and, often, temporary. A shift is immediate. When someone shifts, you'll see it in real time as your conversation, transaction, and interaction progresses. The Talk*SHIFTs* are practical language tools that help you shift not only the words you use, but also your perspective. Many of them can be used to spark a perspective shift in others as well.

TalkSHIFTs are universally effective in business, in families, and in life. In business, they can increase productivity, employee engagement, and business growth. Collectively, the TalkSHIFTs cultivate commitment, connection, and collaboration in personal or professional relationships.

THE WORLD NEEDS A TALKSHIFT (AND WE HAVE THE DATA TO PROVE IT)

Strained and estranged relationships are everywhere in business. Salespeople are frustrated by finance people, customer service and operations people are frustrated by salespeople, and *everyone* is frustrated by IT people.

We have thousands of data points on the TalkSHIFT Assessment, a tool that we'll explore more in TalkSHIFT #2. The data is clear: 72 percent of people have a frustrating relationship at work or at home. Most importantly, people who score in the top 50 percent are twice as likely to report that they have no frustrating relationships than people who score in the bottom 25 percent.

Consider the possibility that the words we use to inspire long-term commitment to our *companies* and coworkers are similar to the words that inspire long-term commitment in families and in marriages.

A NEW LEADERSHIP LANGUAGE

Learning the TalkSHIFTs is like learning a new language. When I opened our business in France, I sought the help of the best business French teacher in Europe according to the *Wall Street Journal Europe*. His name was Jean Luc. I asked him, "How do you learn a new language quickly?"

"Practice the new language everywhere. On the street. At work. At home. Everywhere."

And so it is with the Talk*SHIFTs*. Jean Luc shared another tip with me. He told me to watch movies I love with the subtitles turned on because it helps us translate the words we hear in our head into a new language. Naturally, if you're going to watch a movie a hundred times, choose a movie that you enjoy. I chose *The Usual Suspects* because I have always been fascinated by books and movies that have a twist at the end. The twist makes you want to watch the movie again because you'll see the same movie from a new perspective.

The Talk*SHIFTs* are similar. When you read this book the first time, read it as a business book. When you're done, go back and read it again with someone in your personal life: your wife, your husband, your children, or a parent. What you'll likely discover is that learning this new language together will transform your relationship.

Talk*SHIFTs* create great teams—even when those teams are families.

After all, as Jean-Luc said, "If you want to learn a new language quickly, practice it everywhere. At home. At work. Everywhere."

TOOLS TO FUEL 'THE COMPASSION REVOLUTION' IN BUSINESS

A culture revolution has been brewing in business—Glassdoor's transparency is taming toxic workplaces, LinkedIn is making it easier to find a new workplace, and millennials are demanding a new breed of leadership.

And then, the COVID-19 crisis crashed companies worldwide.

My meeting yesterday was interrupted when a ten-year-old boy popped onto the video window and whispered to the VP of operations, "Could I have a hug?"

As the VP hugged him, I was touched, thinking, "Would this have been okay before COVID-19?" It probably would have been okay in that team because the leader had cultivated a culture of compassion.

Would it have been okay for someone to hug their child in *your* team meetings six months ago? More importantly, will it be okay in your team meetings tomorrow, or six months from now?

Zoom invited our coworkers into our living rooms and our lives—tearing down the walls between our personal and professional worlds.

Will you put the walls back up?

By the time you read this, many will have already had to

make the choice: will I go back to the aggressive way of leading, or will I forge forward to master a new, more compassionate language?

My sincere hope is that we will look back months and years from now and credit COVID-19 as the catalyst for a new era in business—The Compassion Revolution. To sustain this revolution, people will need tools to lead in an unfamiliar way. Without tools to lead with compassion that also result in financial success, many will revert to the primitive, aggressive communication that sustained the last business revolution—The Industrial Revolution.

Compassionate communication is going to be uncomfortable for many people—especially so for aggressive businesspeople like I once was. Those who have the most difficulty will be those who are impatient for change and those who have achieved remarkable success with an aggressive style.

For me, shifting from an aggressive style to a compassionate one was revolutionary. The Talk*SHIFTs* changed me. They changed my father too. If I can change and my father can change, can't your father, your mother, your husband, or your wife change too? What about your boss? Could your boss change?

That is the real Compassion Revolution—the revolution that will ripple out from your team meetings, bouncing off the walls and down the halls into the family rooms of the people in your care.

Here's the thing about revolutions. When you join one, you

never know if you're on the *edge* of something or on the *ledge* of something.

And so, I ask you, "What are you on the edge of?"

I hope it's a Talk*SHIFT*. The world needs a Talk*SHIFT*.

Let's spark one…together.

Beyond employee engagement

The Compassion Revolution has begun.

*Compassionate communication
also gets business results.*

Kenny knows the difference between employee connection and employee engagement:

"Nine months after I started working at my company, I walked into my boss Paul's office. He took one look at me and said, 'Kenny, we've got to get you to the hospital. You've got a huge lump on your neck that wasn't there during our meeting 15 minutes ago.'"

"Let's go," Paul said, and he led Kenny to his car and sped to the nearest hospital. The doctors would later say that

Paul's decision to drive to the hospital rather than wait for an ambulance likely saved Kenny's life. In the short drive to the hospital, the golf-ball-sized lump had grown to the size of a grapefruit.

Through four layers of management, Dylan heard the news about Kenny. They told him, "Kenny is in the hospital with an unknown condition. His fiancée is pregnant. They're not sure if he'll live to see his wedding day in a couple weeks."

Kenny was 24 years old. Dylan recalled interviewing Kenny a year before on a college recruiting trip when Kenny explained that his barely passing grades were a result of a prolonged case a mononucleosis, the impact of which had followed him through college. But Dylan saw something in Kenny: "My spider-sense told me Kenny was a diamond in the rough, and I convinced the VP of the department to take a chance on him."

Paul knew that Kenny was from a rural town and had come to the city for the job opportunity. Dylan, a longtime resident, wanted Kenny to have the best care possible.

Kenny tells it this way: "Dylan called me after I was admitted to the hospital and the situation was pretty serious. Dylan asked, "Kenny, may I have your permission to call the President of the hospital and have him look in on you?"

That afternoon, the Chief Clinical Officer of the hospital came to Kenny's room and recommended a doctor at another hospital nearby who was one of the foremost experts on

Kenny's condition. Kenny agreed to the transfer. As soon as the Chief Clinical Officer left his room, Kenny broke down crying. For the first time, he had hope. The events of that day extended his good fortune in that, nearly ten years later, that doctor who Kenny transferred to still treats him today.

Kenny told me, "We named our daughter Faith because every critical step that led me to the right doctor gave us faith in the future."

Years later, Kenny asked Dylan, "How did you know the President of the hospital?"

Dylan laughed and said, "I didn't. I cold-called him. I left the President a voice mail saying that I had an employee in his hospital and I was concerned that he might need specialized care and might not know the best doctors because he had recently come here for a new job from a rural town with no connections here."

Kenny was released from the hospital—and days later he attended his wedding.

Kenny later commented, "I don't tell a lot of people here my story, because I hadn't been with the company long enough to get disability pay. The company generously made an exception to some of their established policies to allow me to get paid time off during my recovery. I chose to work 60- to 80-hour weeks once I recovered to show my appreciation. When I hear about good employees complaining that the company doesn't care, I seek them out and privately tell them my story. I'm still here—literally—because of the generosity and support from my company and the people who work here."

He said, "Both of the people who saved my life are no longer here, but I am."

That's the power of employee connection.

THE NEW RULES OF (EMPLOYEE) ENGAGEMENT

Employee engagement has been a well-researched and important statistic for nearly 20 years. The Gallup organization's data on employee engagement has been used to build great corporate cultures.

For the most part, the highly engaged people working for companies with great cultures don't leave to work for companies with bad cultures. So, if you're already among the companies leading with employee engagement, how do you compete for talent?

With employee connection.

Dylan isn't the only leader who gets it.

Dylan's actions bring to mind a mentor of mine, Bob Chapman. Bob is the CEO of $3 billion family-owned Barry-Wehmiller. He gets it. In his May 2012 TEDx talk,[1] Bob summarized the guiding principles of leadership that they've been putting into practice since 1988: "We've been paying people for their hands for years, and they would have given us their heads—and their hearts—for free if we had just known how to ask them and said, 'Thank you for sharing.'"

The Compassion Revolution is working for Microsoft too.

Microsoft CEO Satya Nadella is widely credited with transforming Microsoft's corporate culture from cutthroat to compassionate. In the six years since taking over in 2014, Microsoft's share price has increased by nearly 500 percent, creating over $1 *trillion* in shareholder value.

Employee connection doesn't just work for employees—it works for shareholders too.

Thom Bond is the apprentice of and living spokesperson for a quirky psychologist turned peace activist who wrote one of the most influential books you've never heard of. He's one of the pioneers of The Compassion Revolution. Thom is the creator of The Compassion Course online, which has taught over 20,000 people about compassionate communication.

When I interviewed Thom, he asked how Talk*SHIFTs* could give insight into how leaders think.

I told him that many people believe that change must come from the inside out. What makes the Talk*SHIFTs* powerful is that they're tools for changing ourselves *from the outside in*. To shift your words requires that you shift how you think. When you shift how you think, you'll shift your heart. And when you shift your heart, you'll win the hearts of those around you.

The definition of compassion is a bit different depending on which dictionary you consult. Many definitions refer to pity or sympathy, words that typically aren't well received in an office environment. According to the *Oxford English Dictionary*, compassion is when two things converge: (1) a person is moved by the distress of another person, and (2) there is a desire to relieve their distress.[2]

THE TALK*SHIFT*

If compassionate communication is to relieve others' distress, how do we do it? By asking them what they need, like this:

- How can I support you?
- What ideas do you have for ways that I could support you?
- What support from me, from others, or from the organization would be useful to you?

When you begin asking these questions, you will likely find that people may not give you suggestions at first. They may not share with you the support they need because they don't want to "owe you" something or they may be embarrassed to ask for what they most need. Some people are fiercely independent and prefer not to ask for help. And, in extremely stressful situations, the person may simply be too overwhelmed to know what support they need.

When you get started asking this question, it's often helpful to offer the person two or three ideas as a multiple-choice question of sorts, like this:

"How can I support you? For example, we could shift tasks to another team member, adjust deadlines, or take any other suggestions you may have."

When you offer your support, it's important to let go of any expectation that you will get something in return.

Ironically, when you genuinely let go of any expectations, you set yourself up for the reverse *SHIFT*.

THE REVERSE *SHIFT*

What if the person who needs support is *you*? Many of the Talk*SHIFTs* also work in reverse. You can reverse this shift and ask for the support you need, like this:

I have a couple ideas for how you could support me. Would you mind if I share them?

The reverse *SHIFT* here is not a quid pro quo. If you're offering support only to get support, then you're not executing the shift from the right mindset.

Reverse *SHIFTs* are for everyone, including people who don't hold leadership titles. Talk*SHIFTs* are not only used by leaders to "build better bosses—and become one"; you can also use them to *build your current boss into a better one*. Even more important—overachievers, take note here—as a leader in a team, or in a family, when you grant permission to others to use the reverse *SHIFTs* with you, then you'll not only accelerate your own shift but also the shift of those around you.

* * *

Certainly, Kenny benefited from employee connection. And it seems that the company got a great benefit too by having another devoted employee.

Do you know who may benefit most from employee connection?

Dylan said it best.

"I don't know Kenny very well, but I was the only person from the company invited to his wedding. That was almost ten years ago. I don't remember the awards we won that year or my bonus, but I vividly remember Kenny's wedding. I remember his mother hugging me. I remember the tears on her cheek as it pressed against mine. And I remember mine on hers."

So, who benefits *most* from employee connection?

Leaders.

Leaders like you.

TALK*SHIFT* #2

You are (probably) not as self-aware as you think.

According to Harvard Business Review, 95 percent of us think we're self-aware, yet less than 15 percent of us actually are.

"I knew my scores would be good, but not this good," I thought as I opened the envelope and saw my results on Dr. Gerald Bell's leadership assessment.

My score was 199 out of 200.

And then Dr. Bell spoke.

"If your score is close to 200, that's not a good thing."

Uh-oh.

That's how I discovered that my team thought I was a jerk.

Fortunately, I learned this while I was still young. I can only imagine how painful it would have been to learn that I was a jerk decades later. In that moment, I felt like I had spent my entire career walking around with the equivalent of toilet paper stuck to my shoe without knowing it.

My heart started racing. I recall looking at the comments made by the people I worked with every day. In the comments about my strengths as a leader, one of them wrote, "He's young."

I laughed out loud, thinking, "That's great! One of my greatest strengths is something that I'll *outgrow*."

Later, I discovered I wasn't the only one who was blindsided by my results.

According to *Harvard Business Review*, 95 percent of people think they are self-aware, but only 10 to 15 percent actually are. For over 40 years, companies have used 360 assessments to help people identify areas for improvement by soliciting confidential feedback from coworkers.

It seems that most of us have very inaccurate self-perception. Think of it as that odd feeling you had the first time you heard a recording of your voice. It sounded familiar but distorted when compared to how you heard your own voice. Even highly self-aware people are often surprised by confidential feedback. This is because self-awareness is not the same as what psychologists call "other-awareness."

Be prepared to be surprised with the results when you ask

people for confidential feedback about your communication. Whether positive or negative, there is a good chance that your self-awareness and other-awareness are not completely aligned.

I believe that doing a confidential 360 is the single most important activity for every leader. Unfortunately, because of the limitations in execution of most corporate 360 surveys, which focus only on employee feedback, they rarely result in pivotal realizations for leaders.

THE FOLLY OF "FOCUS ON YOUR STRENGTHS"

The "Focus on Strengths" movement gained momentum in 2001 with the publication of *StrengthsFinder* by Tom Rath. The premise was sound—rather than focusing on others' weaknesses, leaders are better served to build on people's strengths.

The problem is that some people have taken the "focus on strengths" philosophy to the extreme—using it as an excuse to dismiss their weaknesses.

I speak with many people who claim to be aware of their weaknesses. They say, "I focus on my strengths, and people around me accept my weaknesses." Really? Are you sure? How certain are you of the degree to which your weaknesses impact others' passion, performance, and respect for you? Consider asking them, "To what degree do my weaknesses impact your passion for your work, your performance, or your respect for me?" Consider the possibility that—while your weaknesses may be "tolerated" because of the end results you achieve—people around you may prefer to work for someone who doesn't generate the stress that your weaknesses create.

You don't need to turn your weaknesses into strengths, but you must neutralize them.

There's another challenge with focusing on our strengths. A strength over-practiced or overly amplified often becomes a weakness.

One strength of many leaders—especially senior executives—is that they are not afraid of conflict. In fact, they often welcome it. They are comfortable being direct and assertive. However, when we are too direct, it often becomes overbearing and domineering. Maybe you've seen a manager or employee who is excellent at a particular skill, but they don't have the patience to wait for others to solve problems and often step in to save the day. The strength: leading the charge to make things happen. The weakness: lack of patience. I often see leaders who ask someone to do something, and when it isn't done quickly enough, they do it themselves. The impact: people may stop taking initiative because the leader has trained them to wait, because the leader will jump in and do it anyway. Often, leaders resist behavior change because they have relied on these strengths that have made them successful in the past. Yet, over time, it is these same strengths amplified that can lead to their downfall in long-term partnerships with key employees and family members.

For example: creativity taken too far often looks like starting lots of projects and finishing nothing. I see this frequently with entrepreneurs and top executives who wear their ADHD tendencies on their sleeve like a badge of honor. They often miscalculate the impact of their weakness on their strength. They tell their team, "Take the good with the bad. My ADHD is also the source of the vision that creates great ideas."

And when those leaders have a new idea, their teams often do nothing. Why? Because they say to each other, "This too shall pass. Next week, he will have a new idea. Let's see if something sticks before we take any action."

Directness was actually one of my perceived strengths at the center of my score of 199 out of 200. I was over-practicing that strength. To successfully grow the company, I relied on attributes I thought were my greatest strengths. These strengths ultimately became a liability as my team grew beyond 30 people. To effectively lead a large team requires partners who are engaged over the course of years or decades. And my directness was burning through some great people. A successful leadership practice in *business* became an unsuccessful practice for leadership in *partnership*.

To help you make this same kind of transition, I've created a tool that you can use to increase your self-awareness while also shifting the communication of others around you.

TAKE THE TALK*SHIFT* ASSESSMENT

The Talk*SHIFT* Assessment was created to solve the problems of many 360 assessments and make it available not only to people in the business world, but to help create stronger partnerships of all kinds, even great families. You can access the full assessment at www.krister.com/assessment. The results are for your eyes only.

When people are not certain that their responses are confidential, they are less likely to give honest feedback. People fear their responses will be seen. For this reason, many HR organizations engage third parties to administer 360s to ensure confidentiality. The Talk*SHIFT* Assessment can be a cost-effective alternative to hiring a third-party administrator.

Because the Talk*SHIFT* Assessment is not administered by HR departments, it can also include feedback from family members. HR departments have too much liability getting that information. Plus, the line between work and family is still drawn in areas of privacy so that idea is currently off the table for corporations. But family members are often the ones who know our weaknesses best. The reason your family is such a crucial addition to this process is because your family members are likely to be the ones who are most honest with you.

One theme I hear frequently from people who approach me after I deliver a keynote is that people are aware that they are "nicer" at the office than they are at home. They say, "I'm just going so hard at work that I come home, let my guard down, and treat my family more harshly than the people at work." But how certain are you that you're nicer at the office?

Consider the possibility that your family just feels safer to tell you than your coworkers do. Or maybe your family feels that they *must* tell you because they have to live with you! Your coworkers just go back to their desks and say to themselves, "Thankfully, I don't have to live with them!"

Feedback from family members about your communication is often the canary in the coal mine that something is amiss with your communication at work.

If you take only one thing away from this book, take the TalkSHIFT Assessment and ask for confidential feedback from at least one person who you believe will give you honest feedback. You'll find the questions on the next page.

As you read through them, some of them may not make sense—yet. But by the time you've finished the book, we will have covered each of them.

THE TALKSHIFT ASSESSMENT QUESTIONS

We're always improving the assessment, so we encourage you to take the most recent version online. For each of the following questions, check the box in the appropriate column for Strongly Agree (SA), Agree (A), Neutral (N), Disagree (D), or Strongly Disagree (SD).

	SA	A	N	D	SD
I wait to share my solutions until after others have offered their suggested solutions.					
I ask questions on a scale of 1 to 10.					
I tend to listen more than I speak.					
I ask questions that begin with the words *What* or *How* rather than *Have you*, *Will you*, *Did you*, or *Are you*.					
When I share my emotions, I name the emotion I'm feeling.					
When I get angry, I identify the emotion behind my anger. Then I share that emotion, rather than anger, with others.					
I listen not only to people's words, but also to the needs behind their words.					
I am aware when I make mistakes or hurt someone's feelings, and I apologize when I do.					
I use requests as an opportunity to give positive feedback.					
I avoid saying the words *you should* and *you need to*.					
When I make a request of someone, I give the person permission to say no and encourage them to share any concerns.					
When interacting with people, I tend to have two (or more) positive interactions for every negative one.					
I avoid saying the words *you always* and *you never*.					
I request feedback and help people to feel comfortable sharing their concerns.					
COUNT OF RESPONSES IN EACH COLUMN					
MULTIPLY BY	**5**	**4**	**3**	**1**	**0.1**
EQUALS					
ADD YOUR FIVE SCORES FOR YOUR TOTAL SCORE					

An **excellent** score is over 63. **Good** is 53 to 63. **Satisfactory** is 48 to 53. If your score is below 48, I suggest that you explore ways to improve, which could be to try the Talk*SHIFTs* in this book. Even if you have an excellent score, you can measure your results against the Talk*SHIFTs* presented here to further improve.

How others score you confidentially is often more important than how you score yourself. When you take the online version of the assessment at www.krister.com/assessment, you can enter the email addresses of people around you and they will receive a weblink to respond confidentially. The more people you get feedback from, the better. Some senior leaders will get feedback from 20 or more people. It's best to get feedback from a variety of sources: coworkers, family members, friends. Once you receive at least five responses, you can compare how you rated yourself with the average of how others rated you. (We require at least five responses to ensure the confidentiality of those who rate you.)

Use the assessment to begin to Talk*SHIFT* with others. The Talk*SHIFT* 360 Assessment was engineered specifically to be a spark that will shift both *your* communication *and* the communication of those around you. Asking for confidential feedback is an indirect way to open a conversation with people around you about Talk*SHIFTs*. When you ask for feedback from others about *your* words, our research shows that most people begin to think about *their* words.

This is by design. Because of the unique language used in the 360 assessment, it can be used to start a shift with your boss, your coworkers, or your spouse. It can even be used with difficult clients.

This is the true power of the Talk*SHIFT* Assessment.

The simple, fill-in-the-blanks phrase for more compassionate communication.

The top business French teacher in Europe taught me to replace this phrase at work. It works in English too.

Most fluent speakers of multiple languages learned foreign languages as children while growing up in a multilingual home. My greatest insights into language, and specifically the language of business leadership, came when I was launching our business in Europe. To be successful, I was required to rapidly learn French and German.

Now, it's no secret that some Americans aren't fans of the French—which I find somewhat ironic because fully 29 percent of the most commonly spoken English words are actually French words. Most English words that end in *-tion*, *-ssion*, *-able*, *-ism*, and *-ive* are French words. It's been that way since the Frenchman William the Conqueror took the British throne after the Norman Invasion of 1066. In the decades that followed, an estimated 10,000 French words were adopted into the English language. For example, both *compassion* and *capitalism* are French words. (Fun trivia: the word *capitalism* may have been coined not by a capitalist, but rather a French anarchist named Pierre-Joseph Proudhon.[3])

A couple weeks after 9/11, I moved to Paris to expand our business in Europe. I had taken six years of French in high school and college. My French was terrible. In fact, it was so bad that when I spoke in French to people on the street, they replied in English. Mastery of a language requires consistent practice. In 2002, I forced myself to practice by leading a three-day workshop in French to teach our software to our newest French customer, the host of the Cannes Film Festival (le Palais des Festivals de Cannes).

The day after the workshop ended, my French salesperson called me to give me the feedback. He started uncomfortably: "Boss, I don't know how to say this, but the client's exact words were, 'Never send him back here again.' Your French is terrible. If we are going to be successful launching our software into the French market, you need to improve your French and do it fast."

Two weeks later, I had my first meeting with my newfound French teacher at his home in Spa, Belgium. A few years before we met, Jean-Luc had been named the best business French teacher in Europe by the *Wall Street Journal Europe*.

Jean-Luc asked, "So what exactly did you say to the people in Cannes?"

I shared with him the French words I'd used.

"And how many times did you say it that way?"

"Over three days? Probably a hundred times," I responded.

He burst into a big Belgian belly laugh. "Let me translate what you just said," he said. "Your French words were condescending. You just lectured the people who host the Cannes Film Festival for three days, saying, 'You MUST do this. You SHOULD do that…' one hundred times."

I didn't intend to lecture them. The realization sunk in that I must have come off as an arrogant jerk. What had seemed to me to be making an effort to speak French in order to fit in was received as annoying and irritating. Plus, my French was so bad that I really wasn't able to represent the product in an understandable way either. Epic fail, or as the French would say, *la loose* (which is, incidentally, taken from the English word *lose* and pronounced the same way).

Jean-Luc said, "We will accelerate your learning by focusing on the 1 percent of the French language that you actually need to be successful in business. Give me the five ways you would say the same thing in English. Then, we will translate your natural words into French to create fill-in-the-blanks phrases you can use. Once you have those key phrases, we will tinker with them and fill in the blanks with different words to create variations for different situations."

The two phrases that I used in Cannes that were most off-putting to the clients were *you must* and *you should*.

Must and *should* are modal verbs. Modal verbs often get us into trouble in sensitive conversations. Without going into an in-depth grammar lesson, modal verbs are used to express subjective attitudes including possibility, ability, probability, desire, obligation, and necessity. The modal verbs to be wary of are *can, must, should, could,* and *would*.

Often, we use modal verbs to make indirect suggestions or judgments. Consider the following:

- You *should* arrive earlier.
- You *could* arrive earlier.
- If you *would* have arrived earlier, we *would* not have been late.
- You *must* arrive earlier.

Note: The phrases *you need to* and *you have to* are not modals, but they are similar to *must* and are best avoided. Obviously, the other words in the sentence can soften or harden the desire or directive but most of the time, these words are "bossy," arrogant, and/or simply annoying.

THE TALK*SHIFT*

The solution to eliminating these modals is quite simple. You can eliminate them or replace them with the word *please* or *consider*.

Replace: "You *should* arrive earlier" with one of these options:

- *Please* arrive earlier.
- *Consider* arriving earlier.
- *Please consider* arriving earlier.

People often use the words *you should* because they have a specific way they want you to behave and feel like they are making a request. The problem is that most people don't want to be directed to behave according to the wishes of someone else. And, when stated this way, we never actually get confirmation from the other person that they agree to comply with our request. So we state the same thing over and over again and often project annoyance into the word choice because we have interpreted our use of *should* as a done deal, when the person who hears it just thinks of it as bossy or annoying. Over time and with repeated frequency, it can produce the feeling of an eye roll (dismissive) or outright rebellion (as in "Who are you to tell me what I should do?"). In these cases, our word choice actually achieves the *opposite* effect of what we seek. Finally, it can bring compliance but result in resentment. I know you may feel that these reactions are extreme, but ongoing use of these words implies a power structure where one is making demands of the other. That is rarely, if ever, a desirable dynamic.

An even more powerful Talk*SHIFT* is to combine a request for commitment, such as:

- How committed are you to arriving earlier next time?
- How open are you to the possibility of arriving early next time?

COMING FULL CERCLE (CIRCLE)

Here's the interesting thing. As I learned better French from Jean Luc, I never applied the techniques to the words I used when I spoke English. Speaking English, my first and native language, comes naturally to me. Later I realized that in business, I could apply the same rules of using better phrases that could be adapted to many situations, all of which would address difficulty in communication. One of the most powerful aspects of Talk*SHIFTs* is that they leverage the best practices that Jean-Luc uses to accelerate how people learn French.

The Talk*SHIFTs* are language tools for respectful and compassionate conversations. People who practice these communication tools find they eventually are used with ease, as with mastery of any new language.

Consider this possibility: your heart may be in the right place, but what if your words are not? As I looked back on my career, I realized that my words were—unintentionally—not aligned with my intentions. My words brought a completely different outcome than the one I greatly desired.

Even the most verbally abusive people often think their heart is in the right place. They often think they are getting it right or they believe they are acting in the best interest by imposing their will on someone else because they see it so clearly or "know it to be true." Yet we rarely see the unintended consequences of how our words are received, especially when there is already a hierarchy in power between people, such as with a boss and a direct report.

ARE YOU LUCKY OR HAPPY?

Stefan was a German on our sales team whose sales territory included the United Kingdom. He was fluent in English and had been selling technology in English for over 20 years when I overheard him speaking with a prospect at a trade show.

Stefan said, "Our customers are very *lucky* with our software."

I cringed, and laughed, while saying, "Stefan is trying to say that our customers are very *happy* with our software. The German word *glucklich* is called a 'false friend' because it translates to both *lucky* and *happy* depending on the context." I gave a sarcastic look. "Unlike the other products on the market, you don't need to be *lucky* in order to be *happy* with *our* software."

I glanced at Stefan, and I could see the wheels turning as he counted the thousands in lost sales commissions because he had been telling prospects for 20 years how *lucky* they would be with the products he sold.

For the next 24 hours, become hyperaware of every time you

hear the words *should* or *need to*—either in your speech or in someone else's. You'll notice that it happens all the time. Once you become aware of it, this shift will become much easier to make.

This is not to say that every time you use the words *should* or *need to* is bad. However, these words are best used intentionally, rather than as a pattern of speech. It is especially important to avoid using them in emotionally charged conversation.

Please stop "shoulding" on yourself and others.

Just like Jean-Luc taught me the shortcuts to learn business French in record time, think of the Talk*SHIFTs* like a shortcut to learning the language of compassionate communication. For this reason, Talk*SHIFTs* are especially appealing to people who speak English as a second language when they are dealing with coworkers or clients from other countries. Talk*SHIFTs* can eliminate many unnecessary conflicts caused by the words we use when translating directly from one language or culture to another.

TALK*SHIFT* **#4**

Let's talk about our words—the ones we're saying—and the ones we aren't.

Get honest answers to difficult questions.

Greg was only 22 years old, and he'd been with the company for less than six months when he first disagreed with me. I could see how afraid he was when he did it. I recall telling him, "Thanks so much for sharing that you disagreed." There were five other young software developers in the room.

At the end of the day, I saw Greg walking to his car. I went up to him and mentioned again, "Hey, it took a lot of courage to tell me that you thought I was wrong. I wanted to say that I really appreciate that. People don't tell me often enough when they think I'm wrong."

I developed more respect for Greg that day than I had for the other employees who agreed with me all the time. Often employees believe that disagreeing with a boss or leader can be a "career-limiting move," but in this instance, it was something that differentiated Greg.

Over the years, I've shared this short anecdote with employees hundreds of times.

Why?

Because a great way of telling people that "it's safe to challenge me" is to share a story about someone who did and how it increased your respect for them.

THE OUCH OF FEEDBACK

"You're a great manager but a terrible leader," Thorsten told me while we were sitting at dinner in Karlsruhe, Germany. Thorsten was the Managing Director of our European division while I was CEO.

My heart raced. I was embarrassed. I gathered myself.

"Thank you for the feedback. I really appreciate that you told me and that you were direct. I recognize that it took a lot of courage to say that, and I want to acknowledge that."

How do you get to a point in your relationships that people are willing to give you such honest and candid feedback?

The first step to establishing safety is to have a conversation about how to have difficult conversations. There are a couple of important elements in this conversation. I used my own tactic of sharing a story about how much respect I had for Greg when he respectfully disagreed with me in a meeting. This can begin establishing safety.

The second thing is to make an explicit commitment that there will be no consequences if the person shares something you don't like. This may be as simple as stating, "I am committed that there will be no penalties for disagreeing with me or giving me honest feedback. In fact, quite the opposite, I intend to encourage and promote honest feedback." Sometimes people perceive our actions as punishment or discouraging, so it can help to address that as well, like this: "I am human. If I'm caught off guard by an especially difficult piece of feedback, I might respond instinctively. A better response is for me to think about it before responding. You have my permission to let me know if my response is defensive or in some way discourages you from offering candid feedback in the future."

Then give the person words to start a conversation where they will share difficult feedback with you. For example, you may say something like this: "If your feedback is especially difficult, I would request that you say, 'I would like to share something that may be difficult for you to hear. When is a good time and place for me to share it with you?'"

If you want to accelerate the process of people feeling safe, then create a situation where you encourage someone to challenge you in a group setting, then offer them appreciation and encouragement in front of the group when they do. A public display of your openness to feedback and being challenged will send a much stronger message to the group than telling them one-on-one that you are open to feedback and being respectfully challenged.

The most important thing when you hear difficult feedback is to encourage it in the moment. Acknowledge and thank the person for their courage. If you are defensive, or worse, aggressive, when someone gives you negative feedback, then you run the risk of shutting down not only them, but all of the people who they tell about their experience. With one slip, you can shut down an entire team.

When you're caught off guard by some especially painful feedback, the best response is simply to thank them and say, "I'd like to think about that for a couple of days. Can I come back to you after I've had a chance to consider it?" If you are feeling comfortable, you may also ask them, "What else can you share with me about your thoughts so that I can think about it more?"

Below are some additional techniques to get honest answers to difficult questions.

Ask before you ask. Before you ask a question that the other person may hesitate to answer honestly, ask whether you can ask it: "Is now a good time to ask a difficult question?"

Prime the response. There's a psychological technique called priming. If you want a more honest answer to an uncomfortable question, immediately precede your question with a priming question like this: "Would you share your honest opinion if it was uncomfortable?" or "Are you comfortable sharing your honest opinions with me?"

Be playful about it. Sports players have signals that they use on the field. You can create a verbal or nonverbal signal that makes it easier for someone to have the courage to address something difficult or negative. It can be anything. One entrepreneur who I coached became aware of his tendency to take meetings off track when he had an idea. He gave his team permission to yell "Squirrel!" whenever he got the team off on a tangent. You can come up with your own fun code word that allows people who are less assertive to start a difficult conversation.

If you are looking for the feedback that is most uncomfortable for others to share, you will have to build up their confidence and encourage them to share smaller bits first. As they share feedback, give positive encouragement along the way, and thank them, saying something like "Wow, that's very helpful. I need to think about that." If they tell you something of which you are already aware, don't say "I know that." If you do, they are less likely to give you other feedback, because they may assume that you know that feedback too. Just thank them for sharing. You may need to build someone's confidence over the course of weeks before they will tell you the feedback that's most difficult to share. It's worth the investment, because it is this sensitive feedback that will lead to transformational changes in your leadership and communication.

THE REVERSE *SHIFT*

You can use many of these tactics in reverse to create safety for yourself. For example, you might ask your boss, "If I had something difficult to share with you, how would you like me to bring up the topic?"

The next Talk*SHIFT* offers a way to calibrate just how open someone is to receiving feedback while checking in on their level of comfort.

On a scale of 1 to 10...

*Calibrated questions that give courage
to those seeking their voice*

Blindfolded, eyes closed, sitting secret-society style in a circle of strangers, an unknown man's hand resting on my left shoulder and my right hand resting on another stranger's shoulder beside me, I hear the facilitator's footsteps walk into the center of the circle. I learn later that he's a CEO by day. Today, he's a volunteer playing a part: part drill sergeant, part compassionate guide.

He speaks. "Raise your left hand if you have ever considered suicide." Wow—that was an unexpected icebreaker.

The man on my right tenses up. As he raises his hand, my hand falls to his shoulder blade. I can feel the echo of his heart beating faster.

The facilitator comes close. His voice softens. He leans in, almost whispering.

"On a scale of 1 to 10, ten being you have a detailed plan on how you would do it, and one being it was a passing thought, how seriously have you considered suicide?"

A long pause.

"Four," he responds.

His body relaxes. It's as if I can feel the relief in his thought: "I'm only a four. Life isn't as hopeless as I thought a moment ago. I'm only a four."

The facilitator delicately hugs the man, holding him tightly. My hand falls away and I hear him as he breaks down, sobbing.

Notice how the facilitator defined the edges of the scale to allow for a wide range of answers that are acceptable and less revealing. By defining 10 as "you have a detailed plan," he frames a continuum with a range of responses that offers a fresh look for the respondent and enables the man to both evaluate and see that he wasn't as close to the end point as he may have thought. As you widen the scope of possible answers with your definition of 1 and 10, you create space for others to defuse negative emotions or negative thoughts.

The power of this approach is that it is one way that those seeking voice can adjust their volume by tempering what they say with some calibration. If this 1- to-10 device works in critical situations like the one above, it can certainly work in a broad range of conversations at the office.

IN THE OFFICE

Imagine your boss asks, "Are our weekly meetings effective?"

Is there really any acceptable answer to this question other than "Yes!" Asking the question in this way creates a cascading effect. If the person answering thinks that the meetings are ineffective, committing to an answer solidifies their mental conclusion that the meetings are ineffective, even if they verbally give another answer.

Now, imagine the boss asking the same question this way: "On a scale of 1 to 10, how effective are our weekly meetings?"

There's a lot more room for honesty when the question is framed that way. You don't feel nearly as vulnerable when responding with, "seven" as you do when you say "no" to such a question.

The more sensitive the question, the more important it is to define 1 and 10 in an extreme way because it widens the spectrum and creates more space for honesty. For example, consider the difference between the question above and this variation: "How effective are our meetings on a scale of 1 to 10 with 10 being the most effective meetings you've ever attended, and 1 being the least effective?"

Now the responder has some information that you can work with. An even more important part of this Talk*SHIFT* is the follow up question: "What does a nine look like for you?" Give time for a response and carefully listen. Then ask, "What do you suggest we start doing, or stop doing, to move closer to a nine?"

Because of the framing of the question, the person is now thinking, "What's the difference between 'the most effective meetings I've ever attended' and this one?" They're mentally already in a good place to provide specific ways to improve the meeting.

THE REVERSE *SHIFT*

You can also use the 1 to 10 to shift a conversation when someone else asks you a difficult question without framing it on a scale of 1 to 10.

Imagine your boss asks you the question "Are you happy with your job?"

You can use 1 to 10 to give yourself more latitude to respond honestly and to lessen any feelings of vulnerability. For example, you might state, "If 10 is 'my dream job' and 1 is the 'worst job on the planet,' I would say that I'm about a six."

If your boss isn't familiar with TalkSHIFTs, they probably also don't know the follow-up question, but you can continue to shift the conversation by asking it rhetorically of yourself. "Six may not sound great, but, since you asked, would you like to know the difference between a six and a nine for me?"

On that scale, a six is pretty good. On the other end of the spectrum, if someone is unhappy, they will likely conclude that this isn't "the worst job on the planet" and an answer of four actually helps them to see some positives in what they have. And it lets them off the hook in truth-telling. The four is completely subjective based on criteria of their own making, with much less risk than a simple yes or no. It is even safer than a version of yes or no such as "not really" for no and "sort of" for yes. Those are just dodgy answers from someone in a panic.

The reason that this shift works is that it gets the person thinking. "Well, I'm not a nine or ten because my boss is a micromanager. I'm not an eight because I don't find the work challenging. And I'm not a seven because my spouse thinks I work too much. So I'm a six. But I can't tell my boss that, so I will say seven." So much more has been accomplished in this exchange and it likely feels more honest to both involved.

*SHIFT*ING PERSPECTIVE WITH 1 TO 10 QUESTIONS

During a recent interview on a popular national radio show, the host and I explored the topic of 1 to 10 questions. I found the interview quite frustrating because the host would interrupt me as I was trying to get my point across. At the end of the interview, the host surprised me by asking, "So, how did I do in this interview on a scale of 1 to 10?"

If he had asked, "What did you think of the interview?" I would have responded, "It was great!" because that's the expected thing to say (and saying "It sucked" is probably not the best way to get invited back!).

When he asked the question, I paused, considering my response. I laughed uncomfortably and asked, "Are we still on air?"

He made a joke: "Well, we do six shows per week and don't have time to edit, but we can edit it out depending on your answer."

The scale of 1 to 10 question emboldened me to be more honest. "Six," I said.

"So, what does a nine look like?" he asked.

"Ahh, the force is strong with this one. You're a fast learner!"

I realized that the problem was not his interviewing style, but that I had not been properly prepared for a radio interview. I was prepared for a podcast interview. The difference is that podcasters tend to allow guests to expand more on their thoughts. Radio and TV, however, tend to be faster paced because they take place within specific time constraints.

His question helped me to realize that I thought the interview was bad was because he was doing the job of a radio interviewer, and he was doing it well. I responded, "Actually, the reason I didn't enjoy the interview was because you got me off script. And now that I think about it, that is what you are trained to do. So, if it's a six, it's not because of you, but because I came into the interview with the wrong expectation."

My perspective shifted.

The construct of the two questions together gives the responder much more to consider and greatly broadens their perspective about possible answers. A simple yes or no is almost always emotion-focused.

When we us this Talk*SHIFT* effectively, it can help the respondent see that the reason something went poorly is actually within their influence or control.

THE SETUP

Some of the Talk*SHIFTs* require some setup before using them. The 1 to 10 technique could be perceived as overly analytical. For that reason, before using this Talk*SHIFT* with certain people, or in certain situations, you may need to establish why you are using this technique. This can be especially important when talking with family or in a conversation that could become emotionally charged.

Simply introduce it as follows:

> I'm going to start asking questions more frequently on a scale of 1 to 10. I've found it's especially helpful when asking sensitive questions. Now, it could be interpreted as if I am trying to be overly analytical, but that's not my intention. The reason I am doing this is because it helps us to have more honest conversations and provides more context for understanding. It also helps to make sure that I am not overestimating, or underestimating, how strongly you feel about something.

You'll find this technique used throughout the book and it is one of the most pivotal Talk*SHIFTs*. I encourage you to practice it and observe how your understanding and connection with others begins to shift. Additionally, using it as a reverse *SHIFT* can open up previously unhelpful questions.

TALK*SHIFT* #6

Listen for needs, not words.

Discover the secret shift of one of the most influential psychologists you've never heard of.

The late Dr. Marshall Rosenberg is another pioneer of The Compassion Revolution. We referred to him indirectly in Talk*SHIFT* #1 when we introduced his apprentice Thom Bond. Dr. Rosenberg is the author of a now obscure book called *Nonviolent Communication*, which is on my top five books of all time list. Originally published as a workbook in the 1970s, *Nonviolent Communication* is a bit of an underground secret. It's sold over 1 million copies, yet it has never appeared on any best-seller lists.

It's also a great book to have handy if you'd like to stop conversations with chatty passengers on airplanes. Just show them the cover when they ask, "What are you reading there, sir? Oh, *Nonviolent Communication*...Have a good flight!"

According to *Fast Company* magazine, *Nonviolent Communication* was the first book that Microsoft CEO Satya Nadella recommended to his top executives after taking on the CEO role.[4] Some credit this book as the catalyst for creating a culture of compassion at Microsoft.

The word *nonviolent* is the direct translation of the Sanskrit word *Ahimsa*, which describes an ancient Indian virtue of "do no harm" that is central to Hinduism and Buddhism. *Ahimsa* is one of those phrases whose meaning was lost in translation when translated to *nonviolent*. *Compassionate* is a more appropriate translation.

One of Dr. Rosenberg's most profound insights involves how our actions (and our words) are driven by a desire to fill our needs. He created a vocabulary of needs (see sidebar).[5] When you listen beyond what people are *saying* and start listening for the *needs* that people are *expressing*, you'll open yourself to a greater understanding of the motivations behind their actions. This helps us to build more compassion and less judgement as we listen. This Talk*SHIFT* is especially powerful when we use it to explore what might be behind the words, attitudes, and behaviors of people who frustrate or incite us.

Imagine the person who criticizes your actions, frequently tells you what you're doing wrong, or rarely acknowledges what you've done right. Consider that their words or lack of appreciation may be more of an indicator of *what they need* rather than a reflection on your actions. Set aside for a moment your reaction to what they are saying about you.

VOCABULARY OF NEEDS

When speaking of needs, it's important that we have a clear vocabulary of psychological needs. Below is the list of core needs.

- Someone's need for **CONNECTION** may be expressed using the words *acceptance, appreciation, belonging, friendship, love, trust, respect, security, stability, support, to understand,* or *to be understood.*

- Someone's need for **AUTONOMY** may be expressed using the words *freedom, independence, space,* or *spontaneity.*

- Someone's need for **HONESTY** may be expressed using the words *authenticity* or *integrity.*

- Someone's need for **PLAY** may be expressed using the words *fun* or *humor.*

- Someone's need for **PEACE** may be expressed using the words *ease, equality, harmony, inspiration,* or *order.*

- Someone's need for **MEANING** may be expressed using the words *awareness, challenge, competence, contribution, creativity, growth,* or *hope.*

- Someone's need for **PHYSICAL WELL-BEING** may be expressed using the words *food, sleep, shelter, sexual expression, safety,* or *touch.*

Instead, ask yourself, "What need are they expressing?" Could it be a need for more respect or appreciation? And why would they need more respect and appreciation? Maybe it's because they don't appreciate themselves, or they don't get appreciation from their boss or others in their life.

Some readers may disagree that it is a leader's job to guess another's needs. There is certainly a danger that I may project my own biases or needs onto another person. For example, if I have a difficult relationship with my boss due to lack of positive feedback, I could project my need for positive feedback onto another person.

The reason why it's important that we learn how to interpret people's possible needs based upon their words is because **many people don't have the language to express their needs**. For many, just saying the words *I need* makes them cringe, because we don't want people to see us as *needy*.

We get fooled into thinking we are expressing needs because we use the word *need*. For example:

- I need you to finish the project tomorrow.
- I need appreciation from my boss.
- I need you to do the dishes.

According to Dr. Rosenberg, the above are not needs. They are strategies to meet needs. The simplest way to determine if you are expressing a need or a strategy is to use the PLATO acronym. If the sentence includes a Person, Location, Action, Time, or Object, then it is likely a strategy, not a need.

For example, "I need appreciation from my boss" expresses

a strategy because it includes a person in the words *from my boss*. Removing *from my boss* turns it into an expression of a basic need: "I need appreciation."

What seems like a minor detail is critically important. Here's why. Once you separate your need from the strategy you use to fill that need, you open up a world of possible strategies to meet that need. For example, your boss is not the only person in the world who can give you appreciation. Do you have a family member or a friend who tends to be more effusive with praise? One strategy for meeting your need for appreciation could be to spend more time with that person.

LANGUAGE CAN BE A GATEWAY TO NEEDS

There's an important language nuance that can help us identify needs.

If I ask someone, "What need are you expressing when you speak a lot in meetings?" they might respond, "I need people to understand where I'm coming from." Or they might say, "Because I need to get to the answers to the important questions we're discussing."

Watch the grammar here. I need *to*. This is not expressing a need. A need is a noun, so it must be the word immediately following the word *need*: as in *I need food. I need autonomy. I need money. I need respect.*

A better way to ask the question is to ask one of the following.

You can use the word *need*, *want*, or *hope* depending on what feels most appropriate in the situation:

- What are you needing more of when you do that?
- When you do that, what are you wanting more of?
- When you do that, I wonder, "What's the deeper need that you are seeking to fill?"

THE NEEDS BEHIND YOUR OWN WORDS

Often, the best place to start listening for needs is to *listen for the needs behind your own words*. You can even listen to the needs behind the words you say to yourself. Take a moment to consider the things you say and do frequently. Look at the list of needs above and ask yourself, "Which of these needs am I meeting for myself when I say or do these things?" Once you've identified the needs, consider whether there are other strategies to meet those needs that will not result in frustration for those around you.

Since I've started listening to the needs behind people's words—and my own—I have one less need myself.

I no longer need an emergency contact.

How to Spark a Talk*SHIFT*

There's a French phrase, *bon courage*, that kept me going on my darkest days. It's one of those phrases where the spirit and meaning gets lost in translation. If you google *bon courage*, you'll discover it means "good luck," but that doesn't begin to capture the inspiration of the phrase.

There's another French phrase, *bonne chance*, that also means "good luck." *Bonne chance* implies good luck when the difference between success or failure will be due to luck.

Bonne chance is what you'd say to someone about to go to the casino. But you would never say *bon courage* to someone going to a casino. Unlike *bonne chance*, the phrase *bon courage* imparts that the difference between your success and failure will be your courage, your heart—your *strength*.

You'll hear the phrase *bon courage* in the mountaintops of the French Alps during the Tour de France. As cyclists climb twelve-thousand-foot mountains, spectators scream *"Bon courage! BON COURAGE!"*

If there is some challenge, some ordeal, some mountain on your path to success, then the phrase *bon courage* applies.

Bon courage is what you'd say to someone attempting to complete an ultramarathon.

A QUESTION OF MILES

Miles had a powerful question for me. I first met Miles thirty miles into my first ultramarathon, about one mile from the finish line (which is, incidentally, the last time you want one more Miles). It was his first ultramarathon too. We exchanged stories about how we had each decided to complete an ultramarathon. I told him that I had been overweight most of my adult life, and that, two months prior, I had never run more than a 5K.

By this time, we were walking. He asked, "What would you have said if, two months ago, someone had told you that you'd finish an ultramarathon today?"

I replied, "I would have said, that's the version of me that I'd be dying to meet."

He said, "You know what happens when you become the version of yourself that you are dying to meet?"

I paused and said, "What?"

"When you become the version of yourself that you've been dying to meet, other people in your life will be dying to meet that version of you too," he said.

Pause and consider for a moment:

Who is the version of you that *you* are dying to meet? Who is the version of you that your spouse, your coworkers, or your children are dying to meet?

You might only be two months away from meeting that person.

The next day, I was in serious pain. In the airport, there was a bodywork place. If you've ever been to one of these places, you'll know they ask you to complete some paperwork. I'm filling out the paperwork and the form has a picture of the body, asking me to circle where I have pain. I circle my legs, my back, my calves. Is there an option for *ALL*?

And then I flip the page.

And there's the question again at the bottom of the form: *Who is your emergency contact?*

My eyes welled up with tears.

And I wrote down my father's name.

The Talk*SHIFTs* transformed my relationship with my father. They can work for you—or someone you know who's struggling—too.

Who in your life—or in your world—is struggling in a business or personal relationship?

What relationship do you have that needs a Talk*SHIFT*?

SPARK A TALK*SHIFT* IN *YOUR* WORLD

As we continue our journey into the Talk*SHIFTs* that apply in business (called the Leader *SHIFTs*) and the ones that apply outside of business (called the Partner *SHIFTs*), please imagine two people. The first person is someone at work with whom you'd like to improve your communication. The second person is someone outside of work—often a family member.

As you continue reading, you'll likely have moments where you'll think, "I wish *<insert person's name>* knew about this Talk*SHIFT*!"

When that happens, here's what you can do to introduce them to a specific Talk*SHIFT*. Each chapter has a corresponding web page where you can share that specific chapter with people in your life. For example, if you want to introduce someone to the concept of the scale of 1 to 10 questions covered in Talk*SHIFT* #5, visit www.krister.com/5 to share that chapter. Regardless of which chapter you share, I'd suggest adding the following question to your email to begin the conversation: "On a scale of 1 to 10, how open would you be experimenting with this technique in our communication?"

It's the easiest way to spark a Talk*SHIFT* with a specific person in your life.

Your journey to sparking a Talk*SHIFT* begins with the first step.

Take the first step.

PART 2

—

THE LEADER
SHIFTS

**Tools to Build Better Bosses—
and Become One**

The three-word secret to inspiring people.

The fill-in-the-blanks phrase to create a
vision that inspires people to follow

Matthew Porter grew up in a fractured family. Abandoned by his birth father, he was raised in a troubled home plagued by dysfunction, drama, and worse. Often bullied as a child for his weight, he was called "Fatty Matty," and he continued to be overweight well into adulthood.

In September 2014, he was diagnosed with multiple sclerosis. His doctor told him, "You have more than thirty lesions on your brain and spine. I honestly don't know how you're able to walk right now."

Four years after being diagnosed with multiple sclerosis, he completed the Leadville Trail 100. After nearly thirty grueling hours, he limped across the finish line to the cheers and tears of hundreds of spectators. His inspiring race was chronicled in real time on the internet, and his last-minute fundraising campaign raised over $50,000 for MS research.

The next day, messages of congratulations poured in from around the world.

He also received hate mail.

One of those letters was from Michelle. She'd been diagnosed with terminal cancer.

Her regret dripped from the page like tears. "Ten years ago, I was diagnosed with terminal cancer. I gave up on life. I've been sitting in my house waiting to die ever since."

"You stole my excuses," Michelle wrote.

Matthew Porter didn't just steal Michelle's excuses.

He stole my excuses.

He may have stolen yours too.

In Leadville, Matthew's volunteer race crew was twice the size of those of many of the professional athletes in the race. People were inspired by Matthew. They wanted to be a part of something larger than themselves and to help him fulfill his dream.

The three-word secret to inspiring people is this:

DO. SOMETHING. INSPIRING.

Matthew didn't have the largest volunteer crew in Leadville because he had already done something inspiring. He made a credible commitment to do something inspiring. That's why people chose to share his vision and become a part of the dream. Once you set a big goal and tell people, the first weeks or months are critical to establishing that there's a possibility that you will achieve this goal. Creating credibility is about creating a track record (pun unintentional) of success. We set a big, inspiring goal and immediately start following it with little wins. In Matthew's case, his journey to the 104-mile ultramarathon started with a 10K, then a half-marathon, then a marathon, and so on.

THE TALK*SHIFT*

Before we explore how to inspire people, let's clarify what inspiration is. The word *inspire* is derived from the Old French word *inspirer*. It evolved into Middle English as the word *enspire*, which meant "to breathe life into." Going further back, the Greek word for inspire was used in the earliest version of the Bible: "And the Lord God formed man of the dust of the ground, and breathed into his nostrils the breath of life; and man became a living soul" (Genesis 2:7).

To inspire is not to motivate. To motivate someone is "to give someone a cause or reason to act." You can motivate people with money, with fear, but you're unlikely to inspire someone with fear or money.

Inspirers ask questions that lead people to breathe life into themselves. People like Matthew breathe life into others with their actions. But the reason why stories like Matthew's inspire us is because his story screams at us a deafening—yet unspoken—question: "If someone with multiple sclerosis is capable of running one of the most grueling ultramarathons in the world, what are *you* capable of?"

Matthew could give you the answer "You should run an ultramarathon."

Would that breathe life into you?

Probably not.

Why? Because answers (may) change minds, but questions change hearts.

Instead of saying "You should do an ultramarathon," Matthew asked me the question that is the basis for this Talk*SHIFT*. In this case, he didn't frame it as a question, but rather as a fill-in-the-blanks phrase.

Write down the following sentence and fill in the blank:

If I were ten times more courageous than I am, I would _____.

This fill-in-the-blanks approach achieves a similar result as asking, "If you were ten times more courageous that you are, what would you do?" However, it can be subliminally more effective because filling in the blank can trick the subconscious mind. The subconscious mind hears the ending of the sentence more loudly than the beginning. Thus, it hears *I would* _____ more loudly than the caveat *if I were ten times more courageous than I am.*

Sometimes, our initial thought when asked this question is negative. If you respond to this question from a negative frame of mind, you may find yourself thinking something like "I'd tell my boss to go to hell" or "I'd file for divorce."

And that is why it's important to ask the follow-up question:

> How would that inspire others in your life? Close your eyes for a moment and imagine you are living 30 years from now. You're sitting with your children or grandchildren, telling them the story of what you are about to do in the coming days or months. What is the inspiring story that you are going to tell them?

Asking in this way will typically help people to think in a more positive light if their initial response is negative.

Now, once people have set their inspiring goal, one of the most common reasons why they don't move forward with it is because they don't believe in themselves. They often don't think they are courageous enough. If you asked Matthew if he thinks that he is courageous or inspiring, he would be the first to tell you that he does not see himself as a particularly courageous or inspiring person.

We often need someone—a leader, a spouse, a parent, or

a mentor—to help us see for ourselves how inspiring and courageous we actually are. When we help people to see how inspiring and courageous they actually are, we *en*-courage them, or "breathe courage into" someone.

To breathe courage into someone, we get them thinking and telling the story of the times in their life when they were courageous:

"Tell me something courageous you did that you are most proud of. Or maybe it's something courageous in the sense that it was adventurous, or you withstood adversity. Maybe it's a time when you stood up for yourself or someone else, or you followed your heart or intuition. Tell me about what you're most proud of."

You'll notice that, in the query above, we plant multiple definitions of courage to give people different things to grab onto. As people begin telling their story, they will likely start telling their story like an observer. Encourage them to tell you in the present tense, as if it was happening in that very moment, like this:

"What was the moment when you felt most proud? Tell me about that one moment as if it's happening right now."

When they tell you their story, hold up a mirror with your words that allows them to see how courageous they are: "Wow, that's an amazing story. Thank you for sharing it with me."

Now you've done your best to breathe courage into them, and we can start talking about the barriers to achieving this courageous goal.

Usually, what happens next is that we begin to think of all the barriers to achieving that vision. And here it can be helpful to ask some clarifying questions to help people to see their barriers. You'll note that some of these questions will help bring people to think more about what's holding them back:

- What excuses are you using to avoid living your best life?
- What is stopping you? In what ways are you stopping yourself?
- Who are you hiding from? (It's okay to answer "myself.")
- What are you hiding from or hiding behind?

Here's the magic. They actually don't have to answer.

Stay silent for two seconds to let them absorb the question. Don't press them to respond. Often they'll have their response in mind within a split second, but they won't be comfortable speaking it aloud.

The best questions don't need be answered aloud to breathe life into people. You can change someone's thinking, even the course of their life, by simply asking a question.

QUESTIONS THAT ECHO

Shortly after that day at the YMCA, I met with my CEO coach, and he asked me a profound question.

He asked, "Are you inspired by your life?"

That got my attention. I knew the answer, *No*, but I never said it aloud.

The question echoed in my mind for three years: *are you inspired by your life?*

I finally found my answer when I crossed the finish line of my first ultramarathon…after Matthew Porter inspired me to do one.

Some of the Talk*SHIFTs* may feel uncomfortable at first. You may be thinking as you read, "I can't say that!" When you find yourself hesitating due to fear, I encourage you to complete the following sentence:

If I were ten times more courageous than I am, I would _____.

An enthusiastic YES requires permission to say NO.

*To get greater commitment, give
people permission to say NO.*

We all want the ease of having others do what it is that we
want them to do. Of course, you get how selfish or self-
serving that is, right? The word *yes* encompasses so much
because the only real yes is an enthusiastic one.

Before you make a request, honestly ask yourself if you
are truly open to the other person declining your request.
Granting permission to decline is a fundamental difference
between demanding something and requesting something.
If it can't be declined, it's not a request but a demand.

Think of requests and demands as two separate tools in

your tool kit. There are times when a demand is appropriate because it's something that must be done by the person you're asking. However, too often we make demands that would be much more effective as requests. Over time, demands tend to increase resentment and erode someone's willingness to give an enthusiastic yes in the future.

There's also a difference between requests and delegation. Because leaders delegate to people who report to them, delegation is frequently seen by the recipient as a demand, when slight changes to the words used can convert it to a request. Further, making effective requests is a skill that works both at work and at home. Have you ever tried to delegate something to a family member? How did that work out for you?

Saying yes to a request sets up a reciprocal arrangement, one that is based on willingness and desire to work together for the good of the team or the relationship. In fact, in some cases, we say yes enthusiastically, not because we want to perform the request but because we value the relationship. Fulfilling requests—especially ones that we don't want to—is a relationship builder. When we are performing a request out of a desire to contribute to the good of the team or the relationship, it's important to acknowledge it with something like this:

- I would prefer not to do this, but I'm happy to do it for the good of the team.
- I'd rather not, but I will do it because I value you and our relationship.

Requests and demands serve different purposes. Neither is better or worse than the other. The most important distinction is to ensure that, when making a request, you truly are granting permission to decline, without fear of retribution or bad feelings. Permission is a critical component of compassionate leadership.

Many leaders never consider that someone might want to decline their request. Others feel entitled as the leader to have what they want, when they want it. Others simply never learned the fine art of making a request. If you're an assertive or dominant leader, you're likely more comfortable with demands. Making requests will be uncomfortable at first. Requests can seem touchy-feely. You may fear that your people will see you as a weak leader or take advantage of you when you practice making a request.

Like any new tool, making requests requires practice before you'll become comfortable using the tool. To experience the power of making sincere requests, commit to experimenting with them for the next two weeks. At first, simply notice how many outright demands you make and the words you use when you make demands. Second, tune in to how you phrase your requests and be honest with yourself if a "no" response would be fine with you. Of course, be aware that a "no" response could look like "Gee, I really wish I could, but there is this other really pressing thing I have to do," because when people don't feel entirely safe, they are not going to use the words *no* or *I can't* without feeling like it reflects negatively on them.

Now that you have a baseline understanding of how frequently you make demands and requests, let's take it to the next step.

HOW TO MAKE REQUESTS[6]

Ask for help. The first step to making a request is to simply ask for help. Asking for help is much more effective than diving into a request because it calls on a person's natural kindness and desire to help. There's an element of vulnerability that comes with asking for help—you are bringing them onto an equal level with you. Depending on your tone and the level of your need, you may even be putting them above you. Say this:

- I need your help.
- Could you help me?

If their answer is "Yes" or a move in that direction, such as the response "What do you need?" then reply with a one-sentence explanation of your request, but keep it very short. At this point, you want to give enough context to explain why you've chosen them and get an initial sense of their willingness level. You can explain the task in detail later.

- I need your help with _____.
- I need your help with a technical project.
- I need your help with some scheduling tasks.
- I need your help with a challenge with a customer.

Explain why you chose them. Making a request is a great

opportunity to give positive feedback or let the person know you've been listening. Here are some suggestions to consider:

- I am asking you because I recall you said "_____" when we spoke last month.
- I am asking you because you are very good at this task.
- I am asking you because you have expressed interest in this area.
- I am asking you because I know that I can trust you.
- I am asking you because this seems aligned with your professional goals.

Be clear on the positives and negatives. If there are any negatives associated with your request, make sure to explain them up front. Also explain the positives. For example, "This will position you for the promotion you're seeking, but the promotion isn't guaranteed. This will likely require an extra five hours per week for the next three months."

Grant permission to say no. If you make it easy for people to say no, then you have more time to spend with people who are open to saying yes.

In sensitive situations, it's better to be more direct about the conditions and parameters of the permission for saying no. For example, you can set the tone of the conversation: "I want you to know that it's okay to say no or to say 'I'd like to think about it for a couple days.' If you aren't interested in doing this, I would rather know where you stand so I can explore other options.

Make it easy to say no by giving them a prepackaged negative response that you think applies to them. In doing so, you are providing the *negative response*, and all they have to do is confirm. For example: "I know you've got a lot of stress right now, so I can imagine now isn't a good time. We've got a busy week, so I understand if you'd prefer to wait until next week."

You've given them a soft landing if they do decide to say no, and now they can relax into hearing and considering your request.

WHAT TO DO WHEN SOMEONE SAYS NO

When someone says no, the most important thing is to give them positive feedback, so they know it's okay to say no in the future. Respond with something similar to this: "Thank you for being honest. It takes courage to say no, and I respect that."

Just because someone declines at this point doesn't mean you won't ask them to do it anyway. While giving permission, you may say, "If you decline, I will explore other options, but there's a possibility that the other options won't be workable. If that becomes the case, I may ask you to do it anyway, but before I ask you to do something you aren't interested in doing, I promise to genuinely explore other options."

The worst thing you can do is push the issue at that time or give them negative feedback for saying no. If you do, not only will that person believe you weren't genuinely granting them permission to say no, but they will likely tell their colleagues that you don't mean it when you say the same to them.

Ask for acceptance of the request. Now that you've established that they can say no, you're ready to get an answer.

You can ask for acceptance in either a direct or indirect way, depending on the situation. If it's important that the person is truly on board with the request, then you may consider using a more indirect approach.

- Do you want to help?
- Would you consider helping?
- Would you be willing to help?
- Would you be open to considering helping? (softest option)

Asking on a scale of one to ten also makes it easier to decline or get a sense of someone's commitment level.

- How interested are you to do this, on a scale of one to ten?
- How excited are you to do this, on a scale of one to ten?
- How committed are you to this, on a scale of one to ten?

Or combine all of the above into a single question: How interested, excited, or committed are you to this project?

Declining a request from a boss is difficult for many employees. When you use multiple adjectives in a single question like the one above, it gives people more ways to say yes (or no). The person might be highly committed but not excited or interested. On the other hand, if they are excited or interested, then they are usually committed. As a leader, you might not care as long as they are either excited, interested, or committed. To take this tactic further, you may add the scale of 1 to 10:

> How interested, excited, or committed are you to this project *on a scale of one to ten?*

And this can tell you more about where they really are with their commitment, such as "I'm not that excited about taking on extra work right not, but I'm very committed to helping you." That gives you a lot of information to work with, and you may acknowledge their willingness to help but really prefer to move on to someone who might be more excited or interested in the task.

As you become skilled at making requests, you'll find that people will be more excited about accepting your requests. Broadly speaking, granting permission to say NO is just one way to grant people more autonomy.

An "Autonomy Raise" is often more effective than a pay raise.

*If you're frustrated by a micromanager—
or accused of being one—use these
tools to shift the conversation.*

You don't have to have the word *manager* on your business card to be labeled a micromanager. Maybe you're coordinating a project where you ask peers to perform tasks, or maybe you're just the one who others call a "control freak" when you're not around.

Micromanagers are often the last to know when people think they are being micromanaged. For many experienced people, it is a long-developed habit, and they are often no longer aware of the extent to which others feel micromanaged. Daniel Pink reveals in his book *Drive: The Surprising*

Truth About What Motivates Us that once an employee's basic financial needs are met (which, in the US, is roughly $75,000), autonomy becomes a primary driver of motivation and engagement.

What is autonomy? Autonomy is freedom from external control or influence. Autonomy is not delegation. Delegation is authorizing someone to do something on your behalf. When people feel a sense of autonomy, it brings a sense of being able to do something in our own way with both ownership and authority over the process. Often when we delegate something, we stay tethered to the how, what, and when of it without truly handing it off.

Even if you believe that you're not a micromanager (aka "control freak"), it can be valuable to validate your assumption. Ask others one of the questions below. The first example may be more appropriate to ask someone who you manage, and the second example may be more appropriate to ask a peer (or family member):

- On a scale of 1 to 10, to what extent do you have the autonomy required to do your best work?
- On a scale of 1 to 10, to what extent would you say that I'm comfortable letting go of control?

Increasing autonomy frees up the leader to move on to other activities. When autonomy is granted as a result of proven performance, it's a way for a leader to show confidence in an employee's skill and judgment, essentially saying "You've got this."

Further, I find autonomy to be the key to retaining top performers, even more than financial incentives. Top performers will get raises and promotions anyway (if not in your organization, then they'll get them somewhere else), so the level of autonomy granted by their boss can be a major differentiator in whether they stay or go.

Even more important than the number that an employee gives you in their answer of rating 1-10 are the answers to these follow-up questions:

- What do you suggest that I start or stop doing to increase your autonomy?
- What does micromanagement look like to you?
- Can you share examples of micromanagement from your work with others—or our work together?

To create extra safety for honest answers, you may preface the question with the following: "I'm working on increasing the level of autonomy that I grant the people who I trust. I wonder if there are areas where I'm micromanaging without even knowing it. I'd like your help to explore ways to expand your autonomy."

This approach allows both leader and employee to co-create boundaries and identify reasonable check-ins and reporting.

CREATE AN AUTONOMY TABLE

The first step to granting more autonomy is to get clear on what level of autonomy has been granted. What's surprising is that many companies already have a model in place to set clear boundaries on authority but don't apply it in other areas. Large companies often have formalized spending levels granted to each employee through their purchasing systems. For example, a Director may have the authorization to spend up to $1,000 without approval, whereas a Vice President may have authorization to spend up to $5,000. There is an ease around this because it is established and well defined and in no way reflects at any time on an individual's judgment; it is merely a standard that has been set. Of course, this is popularly joked about through an expression—"That's above my pay grade"—which relates to very specific guidelines and responsibilities that government employees work within.

Here's a template for what an autonomy table may look like for a project manager:

Provide status updates *weekly* for projects with a budget over *$50,000*.

Provide status updates *monthly* for projects
with a budget less than *$10,000*.

If problems arise in the areas of _____, _____, or _____,
move forward with your solutions and give an update on the results.

If problems arise in the areas of _____, _____,
or _____, present suggested resolutions to your
manager and get approval before taking action.

Get approval for budget variances that may exceed
$5,000 (or *20 percent* of total project budget).

To create an autonomy table for a given role, consider the following questions:

- What are the most important activities that are often the difference between success and failure in this role?
- In what activities does this person have a proven track record of excelling? (As people develop a track record of success in a certain area, grant them more autonomy.)
- What decisions or actions always require your approval in all cases?
- What decisions or actions *rarely* require your approval? What are the exceptions?

After you've defined the autonomy table, you can ask, "In what ways is this less or more autonomy than you've had in the past?" and "In what areas would you like to have more autonomy?"

The autonomy table can be an email. It's also not something that needs to be the same for every employee on a team. Once the template is established, it is easy to change over time.

Employees and leaders at all levels would benefit from a similar outline of the autonomy that's been granted. It serves two purposes: (1) it establishes a baseline that can be reviewed and "raised" as a nonfinancial incentive, and (2) it helps managers to resist the urge to micromanage.

MASTERING MICROMANAGEMENT

Once you've agreed upon the appropriate level of autonomy, it's also important to explore the circumstances when autonomy will be reduced. If this isn't explicitly discussed, you run the risk that the other person will conclude you're a micromanager, thus reducing their commitment to the tasks at hand. Here's a way to introduce the conversation about reducing autonomy:

"I'm ultimately held accountable for the end result. If you were in my position, under what circumstances would you agree that it's appropriate for me to monitor your activities more closely?"

As leaders, when we micromanage, we are sending the message "I don't trust you. I don't think I can rely on you. I don't think you are able to do this without my advice or help."

However, micromanagement is not always a bad thing. There are times when leaders need to micromanage, especially in tense or mission-critical situations where mistakes mean millions. The problem is that we often micromanage unconsciously—out of fear—in situations where micromanagement isn't necessary. And, if left unchecked, this can become a management style or habit. The key is to micromanage on purpose and to set your own boundaries so that it is a temporary measure for a specific purpose and time period. But how do we make micromanagement a conscious act, rather than an unconscious one?

GRANTING PERMISSION TO CONFRONT

Leaders are likely to cross the boundaries of autonomy when under pressure to perform, increasing their own stress and activating a fear response. It's important to grant people permission to share with you if they perceive that you have crossed an autonomy boundary. Here's one way that you can grant permission: "I would like for you to let me know if you feel that I am overstepping the boundaries we've defined. It's likely that we will have different interpretations of these boundaries at times. My responsibility is to honor these boundaries, and your responsibility is to tell me when I overstep them."

Once you've established the boundaries in this way, you have created a shared responsibility for raising someone's autonomy.

THE REVERSE *SHIFT*

Many micromanagers are unaware that they're perceived as micromanaging. If you perceive that you're being micro-managed, begin with the assumption that your boss is not aware of it. In this case, there are a couple questions you can ask to start a conversation that may lead to more autonomy.

If you would like more autonomy, you can use the same approach in reverse to start a conversation about autonomy with your boss. You can start the conversation with "On a scale of 1 to 10, how much autonomy do you think I have?" After they respond, you can share your answer on the same scale. Next, you can use the questions in the autonomy table to identify some specific areas where you would like to request more autonomy.

One reason your boss may not be granting autonomy may

simply be out of habit, or it may be out of an effort to treat everyone equally. Often, it is because of their own stress level or some degree of fear. To help defuse their fear, you may ask, "What tasks do you feel most comfortable that I can do effectively without regular guidance?"

Another likely possibility is that your boss has an issue with your performance that they have not shared with you. You can surface any issues with the question "On a scale of 1 to 10, how comfortable are you that I can do [*insert task*] effectively without supervision?" Sometimes, a leader micromanages because they don't have evidence to feel comfortable that you are capable of doing the task on your own. In this case, you may suggest, "How could I show you evidence that will increase your comfort level in this area? What tasks could we carve out that would allow me to come to you with solutions and prove that I require less supervision?"

Once you've worked with your manager to outline areas to increase your autonomy, you may ask permission to let him or her know if you would like more: "How would you like me to let you know if there are other areas where I can take more responsibility?"

GIVE AUTONOMY RAISES

Why not give your best people an autonomy raise?

For many of them, the autonomy raise will be more meaningful than a pay raise.

Once you have your autonomy tables in place, you can revisit them on an ongoing basis to give your people an autonomy raise. Just like a pay raise, use an autonomy raise to motivate top performers: "If you achieve your budget objectives this year, we can raise your autonomy in this area."

A simple way to grant more autonomy—or demonstrate trust—is to reduce the frequency of progress updates in a specific area. If a project is going well, you may move from weekly progress updates to monthly updates, or from monthly to quarterly. This not only frees up your time as the leader, but it tells your people that you trust and depend on them to do a great job.

Tell people you trust them.

Then trust them.

How to bridge the goal gap.

A conversation template to stop setting stretch goals and start achieving them

Many of the Talk*SHIFT*s deal with engaging your top performers, so critical to overall success. Shared goals may be one of the most important communication skills you can bring to performance. The key with top performers is to co-create your goals so there is a shared sense of ownership, without the goal feeling like an assignment or dictation. Even more important is that they feel positively challenged to meet the goal while still believing that the goal can be achieved.

"I want 25 percent growth this year," I said.

The VP of Sales responded, "That's not achievable given the current state of our product."

"That's why you get paid the big bucks. I need you to create a plan to make it happen."

And the conversation ended. We repeated the same conversation countless times over the next two years.

We grew 13 percent that year. And 15 percent the next year. Our relationship deteriorated. He felt he was doing a good job. I didn't. My confidence in him plummeted. What's worse, his confidence in *himself* plummeted too.

The VP of Sales never believed 25 percent growth was possible. It was never a shared goal, but instead one that he felt was pushed on him without any personal belief it could be reached. He wasn't motivated and he underperformed.

Great leaders encourage people to believe in themselves and achieve beyond what they previously thought was possible. I thought the best way to do that was to push people to set their goals higher by telling them the goal I expected them to achieve. My management beliefs at the time were built on the words of motivational speaker Les Brown: "Shoot for the moon. Because if you miss, you'll land among the stars."

Unfortunately, without effective buy-in and implementation, the words of motivational speakers are, well, not very motivational. Setting stretch goals is not enough.

Too often, unrealistic expectations destroy our relationships. The drain on good employees working to achieve unrealistic goals erodes gains made when results and their work are constantly considered to be "not good enough."

SHIFTING GOALPOSTS

Co-creating shared goals allows people to evaluate what they believe they reasonably can do, mixed with inspiration to do better and go beyond what might first come to mind. But how do we inspire people to achieve more than they originally thought possible?

This process works whether you are the leader working with an employee or you work for someone who is pushing goals on you that you perceive as unachievable. As we've done with other TalkSHIFTs, in the latter case you would just reverse the process. When goals are co-created, they are shared goals where both parties are invested.

It begins with the goal. Let's use the example of an annual sales goal, because sales goals usually impact the compensation of one—or both—people in the conversation. This increases the risk that these conversations become emotionally charged.

Agree on failure. It's often easier for leaders and their employees to agree on what failure looks like. So, start with allowing the person to define failure by asking, "What does failure look like?"

Imagine they respond, "Failure would be achieving sales that are 10 percent lower than last year."

If their definition of failure and yours are close, don't argue. Pick your battles. The time to argue is on the definition of success, not failure.

Agree on success. Now let's agree on success, by asking, "What would a reasonable level of success look like? If we were grading our performance on an A to F scale, let's define reasonable success as a B." (Recalling your school days, in the American school system, grading is typically done on an A, B, C, D, F scale, where A is the exceptional, B is above average, C is average, D is needs improvement, and F is failure. Often a plus or minus is added to allow teachers to differentiate performance, where a B+ is almost an A, and B– is close to a C.)

Imagine the employee responds, "I think a 15 percent increase in sales would be a B."

Now follow up with these questions:

- What are the obstacles to achieving 10 percent more?
- What would you need to do differently to achieve 10 percent more?
- Would increasing this goal by 10 percent raise the grade to an A for you?
- What would I—or the organization—need to do to support you to achieve 10 percent more?

If your numbers are close, consider changing 10 percent to 5 percent. If you're further apart, use 15 percent or 25 percent, but don't go higher than 25 percent because it can cause the employee to shut down and simply agree to a goal they don't believe in and never expect to reach.

Agree on overachievement. Now, let's shoot for the moon. Like agreeing upon failure, it's usually relatively easy to agree upon what amazing looks like.

Ask, "What would an A+ look like? Let's imagine that one year from now, we're looking back, and we achieved something that we thought was beyond our reach. What happened? What did you do, what did I do, and what did the organization do that made the impossible possible?"

Then, let them talk through it.

When they run out of ideas, simply say, "And what else happened to take this to a level of amazing results? What else did you do that was entirely within your influence or control?"

When they've run out of ideas, summarize the impact on them: "So, what would be the benefit to you or your family if that happened?"

Now is time to close the emotional deal.

Restate, in *their* words, the benefit to them. Reflect their dreams to them.

"So, imagine that you've achieved your top goal. What would you want? Imagine that promotion or corner office with a view or that award that you've been striving for. Imagine you're driving around in that new car you've been dreaming about or taking that special vacation with a special someone.

"How do you feel?"

Ask them to write it down. To capture the goal, ask them to write it in their words. But don't just ask them to characterize the goal; ask them to write the actions they need to do to bring that goal to life.

Ask them to answer the following questions in an email summarizing the conversation:

- What is the goal that you're committed to accomplishing?
- What do you need to start doing, or stop doing, to achieve this goal?
- What are you committed to doing to realize that goal?
- What do you need from me, or the organization, to realize your commitment?
- What does an A+ look like?
- What would be the benefit to you if we achieve it?
- What dreams would you fulfill if we did?

And that's it. Now, this may seem like a lot of work, but this may be the most important work of the year. If you're setting a goal for 12 months, isn't it worth it to take four to six hours now to solidify the shared commitment to the goal?

At the end of this process, you'll have the goal and the steps needed to achieve it, explained *using the words of the person charged with achieving it*. If the person isn't able to articulate clearly how they will achieve the goal, this is another signal to you that they aren't committed to achieving it, or that they don't have a believable plan in mind to achieve it.

Once you get the email, you can collaborate to co-create not only the final wording of the goal, but the plan to achieve it. Just make sure, as you add your thinking to their document, that you are not forcing a goal that they don't believe is possible. Your work is to help them see the possibility that they can achieve with the support they believe they need to achieve it.

Now, what do we do when people don't achieve their goals?

Unfortunately, many leaders resort to criticism.

Criticism is lazy leadership.

The world's leading researcher on marriage and divorce can teach us a thing or two about leadership at work.

Criticism is one of the communication patterns that is a strong predictor of divorce. Criticism doesn't just erode the quality of marriages over time; it erodes relationships between bosses and employees, as well as relationships between parents and their children.

You met Bob Chapman in Talk*SHIFT* #1. He's the CEO who began The Compassion Revolution in his company in 1988. The following words from his 2012 TEDx talk hit me hard: "Have you ever worked for a company where you do ten things right and you never hear a word, but you do one thing wrong and you never hear the end of it?"

I realized that those words also described *my* leadership style. The most influential leaders in my life had taught me that a leader's job is to tell people what they're doing wrong—and that is how I led. As I thought about it more, I realized, "That's not only how I lead at work, but how I lead in my marriage and with my kids."

I had made criticism and negative feedback my primary means of correcting behavior, neglecting positive feedback almost entirely. I wasn't trying to be harsh. I thought it was my job to find the flaws, but the long-term impacts on employees and in my family were discouragement and frustration.

Bill Gates led that way. Steve Jobs led that way. And my father parented me that way.

In a surprisingly candid interview in *Fast Company* magazine, Microsoft CEO Satya Nadella described Bill Gates this way: "Bill's not the kind of guy who walks into your office and says, 'Hey, great job.' It's like, 'Let me start by telling you the twenty things that are wrong with you today.'" This change from leading with criticism is just one example of the shift to compassionate leadership that Satya Nadella used to unleash the spirit of Microsoft employees and create $1 trillion in shareholder value in 6 short years.

How much growth are you missing out on because of the far-reaching impact of criticism in your organization? In what ways is lazy leadership creating a stranglehold on your employees—or on you?

What about at home? Are you an overly critical, lazy leader in your marriage or with your children?

Criticism is a habit. If you do it at work, you probably do it at home too.

Criticism is often confused with negative feedback. Criticism is making a negative judgment about a person's *character*, while negative feedback is a judgment about a person's *behavior*. Often, we have those two so closely connected in our minds that we don't realize that they are actually separate components. Unfortunately, we are often socialized to link behavior and character together without considering them individually. Behavior can certainly reflect character. But any judgment of character is just that: judgment. Rushing to judgment based on behavior is lazy and creates lazy leadership through the quick connection of the two, so much so that behavior and character become hard to separate for managers and leaders in an organization.

Giving feedback is part of any leader's responsibility, and the difference between feedback and criticism is often reflected through poor word choices. Leaders—especially first-time managers—are typically promoted based on their expertise, so once they have responsibility for the work of others, they see mistakes that others don't see. How they communicate those mistakes takes the form of feedback or criticism. Add to this that leaders are often stressed or angry and may be struggling with our own issues of wanting everyone to do it the way we prefer, based on our expertise, and when we observe mistakes and shortcomings in the work of others, we likely want to rapidly remedy the situation. That rapid rush to both judgment and remedy can lead to creating a shortcut called criticism. Criticism is all about emotions: yours and theirs. In it, there is a feeling of lack and your emotions about that, which, through your words, transfer to the receiver. In this Talk*SHIFT*, we'll explore a few simple rules to follow in choosing words that are less likely to escalate emotions.

WORDS TO IDENTIFY CRITICISM

Criticism is personal, so watch for times when find yourself saying "You are _____." The blank is filled with a judgmental adjective (e.g. *lazy*, *mean*, *rude*) or a labeling noun (e.g. *a jerk, a typical millennial, an introvert, a slick salesperson*) that is perceived as negative by the listener. This phrase, when coupled with inflection, body language, or a facial expression, can also communicate judgment even when noting a behavior, such as "You are late," which can be perceived by the listener as a criticism. It's important to note the listener may perceive words as negative that the speaker does not perceive as negative.

Sometimes we put softeners in front of it, such as "I feel that you are _____" or "I think that you are _____." This doesn't cushion it at all because you are basically confirming that you are making a judgment. Even more damaging, sometimes a criticism is phrased as a rhetorical question: "Are you _____?"

Do not follow the words *you are* (or the rhetorical version *are you*) with a negative adjective or noun.

Critical statements (criticism) typically focus on who or what someone *is*, and noncritical statements (feedback) focus on what someone *does*.

What if the word after *you are* is a verb? For example, *you are working* or *you are writing*. This is almost always better than following with a negative adjective or noun. If the word after the verb is a negative adverb, this can still be criticism. (Quick grammar school reminder: an adverb typically ends in the letters -*ly* in English.) For example, "You are working lazily" is just as destructive as "You are lazy." In other cases, similes can be used to criticize. A simile typically starts with the word *like*, as in "You are talking like a jerk."

Equally important to watching your usage of *you are* is to watch for the words **always** and **never**. When we couple the words *always* or *never* with a behavior, it converts feedback into criticism. For example, "You are always late" or "You never finish projects on time." When we project that some-one does (or doesn't do) something 100 percent of the time, it is perceived as a reflection on their character. It likely isn't correct, either, and typically is used when we're frustrated, angry, or feel put upon in some way. In other words, it is often used in reaction to some emotion we are feeling rather than in an attempt to give helpful feedback.

Eliminate using the words *always* and *never*.

Although we've focused on how critical language shows up in direct conversations with others, it's also important to increase our awareness of the critical language we use when talking about people who aren't in the room. If we, as leaders, use critical language about others while in conversation with our people, then we model the use of critical language, and it becomes contagious. Again, it is lazy because it just piles on and creates a prevailing attitude about *someone*. Most team members will watch for how much criticism is tolerated or encouraged, so it is important that all leaders focus on feedback based on behavior, not criticisms about people. You are modeling critical language for others even if you replace the words *you are* in the examples above with any of the following: *he is*, *she is*, *they are*, *that team is*, followed by any negative statement.

THE SOURCE OF CRITICISM

As I explored the underlying drivers of my own criticism habit, I learned that it was driven by a deep feeling of inadequacy that resulted from years of criticism from my father. We often use criticism to make ourselves feel bigger—by making others feel small. The real result is that both people end up feeling small.

Many people live beneath a cloud of criticism. As a leader, spouse, coworker, mentor, or friend, recognize that your words make an impact on the hole in someone's soul created by ongoing criticism from a parent, spouse, or former boss.

Growing up in a family business gives me a unique perspective on the intersection of leadership as a parent and leadership in business. For me, there was no separation of the two.

Now, you might not work for a family business, but you likely know someone who does. Family business is the most prevalent ownership model in the world, accounting for an estimated 70 percent of the world economy. The family business dynamic is the ultimate acid test of leadership in partnership that too often explodes in conflict when roles of father and founder, sister and son, brother and boss, coworkers and kin collide. When family conflict erupts, companies—and the careers created by them—are often incapacitated or, worse, destroyed.

I lived in the shadow of an entrepreneur who cast a constant shadow of criticism—because he wanted me to be the best I could be.

I see President Trump taking credit for his accomplishments in press conferences and, while I know many find this habit infuriating, I look upon it with compassion. While I don't agree with all of his policies, or his rhetoric, I can acknowledge that he was also the son of a larger-than-life entrepreneur. I suspect he too spent much of his life living in a shadow of criticism.

When we live a young life beaten down by criticism, we often look for ways to affirm ourselves. For some, the affirmation comes from business success. But business success cannot fill the hole of pain created when our parents, or leaders, never say "I'm proud of you."

For me, business success was my substitute for lack of encouragement from my father, who was also my boss. How does this show up in your life? What do you use to fill the hole in your soul created by a lack of appreciation or affirmation from the authority figures in your life?

Living in a shadow doesn't only happen in family businesses. Ambitious leaders are everywhere. Some are larger-than-life leaders; others are top performers on the fast track for promotions. Apple and Microsoft are not family businesses, but are were countless leaders who have lived for decades in the shadow of Steve Jobs and Bill Gates.

Who lives in *your* shadow? Do you cast light on them, or shade?

Living in the shadow of another—a boss, a parent, a spouse, a sibling—distorts your self-esteem. If that other person is a parent or a leader who never gives you positive feedback—never acknowledges your light—it can affect you in ways that you may not recognize.

What would become possible if we—and our leaders—focused on casting light instead of shadows?

Great leaders cast great light, not great shadows.

Wise words to acknowledge what went right, even when things go wrong

The reality is that, as leaders, it's difficult to focus only on the positive. Sometimes focusing on the negative comes out of fear. If our team makes mistakes, we could lose our job, right? It's often not practical to focus 100 percent on the positive. When we share the negative parts in the same conversation as the positive parts, people often don't hear the negative.

So the simple fix is just to share the positive and negative in two different conversations, separated by a couple days. As you're beginning to develop your encouragement habit, a simple step you can take is to start with the positive conversation first.

This allows the person to feel recognized and good about the work they do. They feel valued.

Wait to talk later about the areas for improvement. We often feel that we need to couple them together, but if employees feel valued and you easily praise the excellent work they are doing, getting thoughtful insights about an area that needs improvement can grow both your relationship and your business.

In fact, you may discover that you don't need to tell them the negative part at all. Maybe you can just ask them what they think needs to be improved. I recall a time when a key performer spent a couple weeks on an important presentation. He emailed me the first draft. I was fairly busy that day and happened to run into him at another meeting.

I asked, "I know you spent a lot of time on that presentation. What would you improve if you had more time?"

He already knew what needed to be improved. He responded with five very specific improvements that he would make.

I said, "Go ahead and make those improvements and send it to me tomorrow."

Not only was it unnecessary for me to tell him what needed to be improved, but this approach saved me the time that I would have spent reading the report and preparing my comments for him.

Sometimes the most efficient way to identify areas of improvement is simply to ask the other person what *they* would improve.

WHO KNOWS BEST?

Are you always the best person to provide the areas for improvement? In some cases, you may not be the best person to share with someone where they can improve. If you're a parent, you've probably seen that often another parent, a teacher, or a coach is more likely to create change in your child. The same dynamic can also apply in business.

When you're not the right messenger for the message, explore with the person who is, like this:

- Who would be in the best position to help you identify areas for improvement?
- If you were looking for the perfect person to share ideas for improvement in this area, what skills or experience would that person have?

They might respond, "You are the best person." And if they do, they will likely be more open to hearing your insights than they were before you asked the question.

The person doesn't have to be in your organization. Help them to think more broadly by adding the following:

Maybe that person is on another team, or possibly in another organization. It could even be a friend, family member, or acquaintance who you know outside of the organization.

Once they outline the type of person, if they don't know anyone who meets those criteria, maybe you can help connect them with someone who does. How much time does that save you?

Not only do you save time that would have been spent sharing your insights, but you've also connected them to someone who they are more likely to listen to, and who may have more expertise than you. And what's more, if this is an area where that person needs ongoing development, you've created a connection that the person can tap multiple times in the future.

And finally, they say "don't shoot the messenger." You've eliminated the risk of damage to your relationship because you've delegated not only the message, but the role of the messenger!

Now, I am not advocating that you abdicate your role of sharing your insights for improvement with others. Rather than assuming that you, as the leader, must deliver 100 percent of the message, consider that sometimes the message can be delegated to others.

WHAT'S YOUR POSITIVE TO NEGATIVE RATIO?

Understanding our balance of communication is important not only in professional relationships. It's important in personal relationships too. According to Dr. Barbara Fredrickson, author of *Positivity*, 80% of people fall below the 3-to-1 positivity to negativity ratio in their communication with themselves and others. To have flourishing relationships, work to create three positive interactions for every negative one.[7]

To find out if you're effectively balancing positive with negative, ask people around you:

On a scale of 1 to 10, how effectively do I balance the positive and negative, ten being that I deliver a balance that *maximizes* your passion and performance, one being that my current balance of positive to negative reduces your passion and performance?

An excellent way to learn new techniques for delivering areas for improvement in ways that have a positive impact on people is to ask them the following:

- Tell me about a time when you learned about an area of improvement that impacted your performance in a *positive* way. How was that message delivered?
- Tell me about a time when you learned about an area for improvement, but it had a *negative* impact on your performance. How was that message delivered?
- Tell me about someone who brought out the best in you. It could be someone in a work setting or someone in your personal life—a sports coach or personal mentor. What was it about that person that brought out the best in you?

If focusing on the positive doesn't come easily for you, when you ask people the questions above, it will give you ideas that you can use not only with that person, but everyone in your life.

SIMPLE PHRASES TO FOCUS ON THE POSITIVE

The greatest leaders will acknowledge what went right, even when things go wrong. Maybe a project fails, but the person clearly invested a significant amount of time in the project. We can still acknowledge their effort.

Often, we reserve positive words only for the times when people do something heroic or spectacular. To expand our skill in delivering positive news, we can use the following phrases that can be used more often:

- I appreciate it when you _____.
- I'd like to acknowledge you for _____.
- Thank you for _____.

MAKE IT MEMORABLE

Years ago, I started a simple practice that I encourage you to try. Every morning, write down three people for whom you are grateful. Think of the specific actions they did the day before that you appreciated. Think of the impact that these had on you or others. Maybe they saved you time or reduced your stress level.

Then, record a short 15 to 30 second video (or voice memo) on your phone and send it to them. Here's a script that you can use:

> Hey there, I was just reflecting on things that happened yesterday that I'm grateful for. You popped into my mind. I really appreciate [*insert what the person did that you appreciate*]. The impact that it had was [*insert the impact it had on you or others*].

Recording a video is so much more powerful than saying it to the person face-to-face because it gives them something they can keep. You'll be surprised at how many people will tell you—years later—that they listen to your message from time to time. Many people will show their family members.

To prompt that, consider adding the following sentence at the end of your video message:

> I wanted to share this with you personally via video so that you could share it with your own family or friends. Thank you. I really appreciate what you're doing.

Start a conversation with someone in your life about the balance of positive and negative in your communication with each other.

Then start casting your light, instead of your shadow.

Lead people to *their* solutions, not yours.

The difference between leading with questions and asking leading questions— and how to tell the difference

Most leaders equate good leadership with giving their people solutions. I call it leading with solutions. Looking back, this is probably one of my Top 5 mistakes as a leader, father, friend, and husband.

Often, we lead with solutions because having the answers validates us and makes us feel like we're adding something. At the neurochemical level, validation becomes addictive. If someone comes to you with a question, neuroscience shows that you get a dopamine hit when you have the answer. It feels good to go home at the end of the day knowing that the solution you provided saved someone time, or saved them from making a mistake. It validates in some way your feelings of why you are the leader.

Early in your career, leading with solutions gets you promoted. Busy people who are focused on hitting deadlines and doing quality work appreciate being offered solutions that save them time. They love learning from you because they want to learn from your expertise, adding their unique twist to get their own promotions. And people for whom work is not their priority enjoy being led with solutions; it allows them to stop thinking about work problems when they go home, because they expect that you'll solve the problem for them tomorrow anyway.

However, there's a major downside of leading with solutions. There is one group of people who prefer not to be given the solutions.

Top performers—like you.

Top performers don't like being given the answers. Top performers don't copy the answers on the test from the person sitting next to them. They enjoy the process of figuring out their own solutions. When you steal that from them and take the dopamine hit yourself, you are undermining their contribution and overall enjoyment of their work.

To maximize the results of your top performers, stop leading with answers.

Are you working 60+ hours per week, every week, and

receiving hundreds of emails per day? If so, you're almost certainly leading with solutions. If you want to be a leader with balance in your life, then **start leading with questions instead of leading with answers**.

This becomes particularly relevant once you are leading a team larger than twenty people. There's an invisible ceiling somewhere around twenty employees that many leaders don't see. That's the ceiling where leading with answers breaks down. To stay connected to real-world leadership, I coach a handful of CEOs and their executive teams to learn the leadership skills they need to lead hundreds of employees, and I see them bumping up against this ceiling all the time.

The higher you go in an organization, the more damaging it is to the value of your business for your organization to be dependent on you. Your top performers are critical to the success of your company. People tend to work much harder to make their *own* solutions successful. When you lead top performers with solutions, you're harnessing only a small fraction of their potential. You lose both the creative thinking when they come up with their *own* solutions and the extra energy they put into executing their solutions.

Before starting the private equity firm Serent Capital, Kevin Frick spent a decade at the most prestigious consulting firm in the world, McKinsey & Company. Today, Kevin runs his own private equity firm. When he was at McKinsey, he was the guy who the top private equity firms called for advice about what makes good and bad acquisitions.

I interviewed Kevin, and this is what he had to share about CEOs who rely too heavily on leading with solutions. He said, "If a CEO's expertise and relationships are mission critical to a business, then that business is not very resilient because it has a single point of failure. That results in investors discounting the value of the company. The degree of discount can vary from 10 percent to 20 percent at the low end, all the way to 100 percent at the extreme. In other words, in extreme cases, CEOs who lead from expertise are so problematic that we would recommend to our clients to walk away from an investment."

According to *Harvard Business Review*, one of the most popular articles of the past 40 years is an article titled "Who's Got the Monkey?" It describes the case of a manager who always had a line of people outside their door. Employees came in, asked the manager questions, and, in doing so, filled up the manager's plate with work.

Who's leading who? Do you have a line outside your door of people leading *you* with *their* questions? What if leading with solutions isn't leadership at all? Are you performing as just another top performer in your organization?

Questions lead. Answers follow. Are you leading with questions, or are you following with answers?

Hint: if you are thinking any of the following, you are probably leading with solutions.

- I can do this faster if I do it myself.
- I need to train my people to solve problems just like I do.
- If I only had ten people just like me.
- Why does it take him so long to do what I can do much faster?

LEADING WITH SOLUTIONS IN PARTNERSHIP

Leading with solutions doesn't work very well outside of the office either. There's a humorous two-minute viral video called *It's Not About the Nail*[8] that garnered over 20 million views, primarily from frustrated wives worldwide who gleefully shared it with their husbands.

Sometimes, we unconsciously believe that solving someone's problems will cause them to like us—or love us—more.

What usually happens is the opposite. Solving people's problems for them drives them away. Solving their problem sends a subconscious message: "You can't do this yourself. You need me to solve your problems for you." Solving someone's problems may make you feel more secure in the relationship and provide that addictive hit of dopamine we mentioned earlier—but it will slowly erode your relationship.

Solving others' problems puts you in a position of superiority. People may appreciate having their problems solved in the short term, but—over the long term—most people prefer to be in relationships where they feel like equals.

LEADING WITH QUESTIONS VERSUS LEADING QUESTIONS

The most common mistake when shifting away from leading with solutions is to ask questions that lead people to *your* solutions. This happens when we disguise the answer we want to hear as a question.

A conversation with my VP of Customer Service illustrates this point. After I asked him a number of questions, he looked at me in frustration and said, "Krister, you clearly know what you want me to do, so why don't you just tell me?"

The leading questions switch didn't work out so well for me. When we dress up our solutions as questions, this is asking *leading* questions. This is not the same as leading *with* questions.

Solutions disguised as questions almost always have a yes/no answer and begin with the words *did you, do you, have you, are you,* or *will you.*

Disguising solutions as questions is less effective than stating your solutions outright for a number of reasons:

- Asking a question often takes more time because it requires the person to respond.
- If you make a suggestion outright, and they think it is bad suggestion for some reason, it's easier to just disregard and continue the conversation.
- If you disguise your solution as a question, the other person is forced to respond to tell you that they will

not do that, and probably to justify why they won't do it. It creates a dynamic where two people can get locked into convincing each other rather than focusing on new solutions to which both can agree.

THE FINAL STEPS BEFORE GIVING SOLUTIONS

Before providing solutions yourself, you can also use the technique we explored in Talk*SHIFT* #11 about criticism. Maybe there's an even better person than you to provide solutions. Consider asking "Who is the person most qualified to offer you solutions? What experiences or perspective would the best person to offer suggestions have?"

If you are the best person to provide solutions, it's always helpful to ask the person, before giving your solutions, "On a scale of 1 to 10, how open are you to suggestions?" Sometimes, you will have people who resist your suggestions, and simply asking them if they are open to suggestions will open them up.

And finally, before offering your solutions, if your solution seems obvious to you, then practice the **assumption of intelligence: assume that the other person is as intelligent as you are.** The person who is bringing you a problem has likely been thinking about this problem for hours, weeks, or months. If you come up with a solution in five minutes, assume that they have already thought of that solution too! If you offer obvious solutions, you run the risk that the other person will think to themselves, *does my boss think that I'm stupid?*

Here's how practicing the assumption of intelligence looks:

- I assume you've already thought of this, but to what extent have you considered [*insert your solution*]?
- You've probably already thought of this, but my gut reaction is [*insert your solution*].

BREAKING THE HABIT OF LEADING WITH SOLUTIONS

To break the habit of leading with solutions, it helps to retrain your brain to get satisfaction from asking the questions that bring others to solutions. Watch people's faces closely as you ask powerful questions. You'll see the look of delight when they see the answer. Take pleasure in the fact that it was *your* question that brought them to their solution.

If you've been leading with solutions for a long time, you may need to help *others* break the habit of relying on you for solutions rather than thinking of solutions themselves. To shift these habits, be explicit with what you are looking for from the conversation.

Clarify the role that you will play in the conversation by asking the following:

- How can I best support you in this conversation?
- Are you looking for me to give you solutions?
- Are you looking for me to serve as a thinking partner and ask you questions that help you clarify your own thinking and find your own solutions?

- Or perhaps you have a specific solution in mind and you're just seeking my approval and support to deliver that solution?

If you work for a leader who defaults to giving you solutions, reverse the above like this:

I have a problem. I think I have the solution, and what I am looking for from you is...

- approval to move forward and the resources to make it happen
- your suggestions for alternative solutions or improvements to my solution
- a sounding board to ask me questions that may clarify my thinking

Great leaders encourage solutions rather than offering them. Creating a welcoming environment for suggestions and solutions keeps the energy flowing and the ideas coming without getting attached to any single path while exploring possibilities.

The Magic Management 8 Ball.

*Shift your perspective on effective
leadership communication with this
counterintuitive experiment.*

If you're like most effective leaders, you spend a lot of time preparing for meetings by thinking about what you are going to tell people. You think about your goals, write an agenda, and create an outline of your key points.

What if you prepared for meetings not by thinking about what you were going to tell people, but what you were going to ask people?

I don't have time is the most common objection to leading with questions. The assumption is that telling people is faster than asking them. What if leading with questions actually takes *less* time than leading with answers?

You don't need me to prove it to you. The Magic Management 8-Ball Challenge is an experiment that you can do to prove it to yourself.

In the 1950s, Mattel released the Magic 8 Ball, a fortune-telling toy. Kids ask the Magic 8 Ball a yes-or-no question, turn it over, and an answer—such as *Most likely* or *My sources say no*—appears on the surface of the toy.

What if leadership were as easy as the Magic 8 Ball? Inside the Management 8 Ball are not answers, but powerful questions. How much would it reduce your stress level if you could lead people by randomly selecting questions from a list of fifteen powerful questions?

How much mental energy and time does it take to come up with the solutions to others' problems? How much time and mental energy would you save if you had your go-to questions at the ready?

THE MAGIC MANAGEMENT 8-BALL CHALLENGE

And thusly, the Magic Management 8-Ball Challenge was born. Here's how to do it.

Call a meeting with someone to brainstorm solutions about some problem they are having. Before the meeting, pick five questions from the list below. Commit to saying very little in the meeting other than the five questions you select.

Here's the canned list of the Magic Management 8-Ball Challenge questions:

1. So, what's the core issue here? What's the problem behind the problem?
2. What should we start doing, or stop doing?
3. What assumptions are you making that are limiting the solutions you are considering?
4. What support do you need to be successful? In what ways am I, the organization, or other factors outside of your control holding you back?
5. Often the most powerful insights are in the words left unsaid. What do you think has been left unsaid?
6. What important questions have we not yet asked that may change our thinking?
7. If you could wave a magic wand, what outcome would you wish for? What would need to happen to make your wish come true?
8. Which solutions are you considering, and what are the pros and cons of each?
9. What solutions have you eliminated and why?
10. If we were ten times bolder than we are, what would we do?
11. Tell me more. (Let them respond, then ask) Could you expand on that?
12. If this situation was a gift from a higher power to cause you, or us, to learn a profound lesson, what lesson could that be?
13. What's holding you back from doing what you think is right?

14. How committed are you to this solution, on a scale of 1 to 10?
15. What needs to happen to increase your commitment to this solution?

Now, the Magic Management 8 Ball is really just a thought experiment. I'm not recommending that you actually go into a meeting and announce, "I'm going to select a random question from the list."

That might not serve to enhance your credibility in the office! Below are some simple Talk*SHIFT* questioning techniques that will help you ask better questions in the future.

ELIMINATE YES-OR-NO QUESTIONS

Any question that elicits a one-word yes or no is a *closed question*.

To eliminate yes-or-no questions, eliminate questions that start with the words *did you, do you, have you, are you, does he, has she,* or *is she*.

Instead, replace them with questions that start with the words *what* or *how*.

If you start questions with the words *what* or *how*, you will never have to worry about asking leading questions that lead people to your solutions. For example, the following is what David Rock calls a *queggestion*, or a suggestion disguised as a question: *Do you pay salespeople on commission?* Rephrasing it using the words *what* or *how* quickly fixes the problem, like this: *What incentives do you have in place for your salespeople to sell more?* or this: *How do you compensate your salespeople?*

ASK *UN*QUESTIONS

*Un*questions open up the conversation. They can guide someone to the areas that you find most interesting or areas where you really need to know more about the topic.

Tell me more is one technique for asking an *un*question:

- Tell me more about [*repeat part of what the person said*].
- [*Repeat what the person said.*] Interesting. Tell me more about that.

Another way to ask an *un*question is to simply pick out a word—or the last word—from what the person just said and repeat it with a questioning tone.

For example:

> Bob says, "Our biggest customer has a major problem."
> You say, "Problem?"

Another simple *un*question technique is to *wonder* about something. It's a technique often recommended by marriage therapists to soften a question in tense conversations.

It sounds like this:

- I wonder how you compensate your salespeople.
- I wonder what your compensation plan looks like.

One common mistake with *tell me more* or *I wonder* is to follow up these with the words *if* or *why*. *I wonder if* usually takes you to a yes-or-no answer, leading you to dead end. Similarly, *I wonder why* and *tell me more about why* creates challenges that you'll read about below.

UPGRADE WHY QUESTIONS

People make mistakes. It's natural to want to ask them, "Why did this mistake happen?"

But here's the problem with that.

Why questions usually lead to defensiveness. For example, *Why did you do that?* and *Why didn't you call the customer first?* are questions that put people on the defensive.

Asking *why* someone made a mistake focuses on the past. In the future, focus on the future with people. Rather than asking *why* someone screwed up, replace your why questions with what and how questions that will focus on the future and lead to a more engaging dialogue.

- What did you learn from this that will help in the future?
- Knowing what you know now, what would you do differently in the future?
- How would you change your approach in the future?

Why questions aren't always asked when people make mistakes. Sometimes why questions are suggestions in disguise. *Why don't you fire that person?* sounds a lot like a suggestion to fire the salesperson disguised as a question, doesn't it?

Why questions are *everywhere* in business. Here's why.

In the 1930s, Sakichi Toyoda of Toyota Motor Corporation began a practice called the 5 Whys,[9] also commonly referred to as *Root Cause Analysis*. The principle behind the 5 Whys is sound. When presented with a problem, ask *why* five times to get to the root cause of the problem.

Here's an example of traditional root cause analysis:

> Michael isn't hitting his sales quota.
>
> Q: Why?
>
> A: Because Michael doesn't know how to sell.
>
> Q: Why?
>
> A: Because he hasn't been trained.
>
> Q: Why hasn't he been trained?

Root cause analysis is a powerful technique but, developed in the 1930s, it's due for an upgrade. Welcome to *root cause analysis version 2.0.*

Here's root cause analysis version 2.0:

> Michael isn't hitting his sales quota.
>
> Q: Tell me more about what you think is behind that.
>
> A: Because Michael doesn't know how to sell.
>
> Q: Hmm, Michael doesn't know how to sell. Tell me more about that.

Rather than asking why, just repeat their words and add "Tell me more" or "I wonder what's behind that" afterwards.

Asking better questions is just a beginning. The even better skill is really listening to the answers.

TALK*SHIFT* #15

The secret to listening is talking.

To upgrade your listening, upgrade your questions.

Most of us think we're good listeners. Or, if we self-admittedly know we lack these skills, we shrug it off as a bad habit or trait. Rather than listening, our brain is usually fast-forwarding to what we're going to say in response to what is being said rather than actually listening to what is said. This easily leads to misinterpretations and, often, mis-understandings. You may think you're fooling people, but people know when you aren't listening because your reply or next comment has nothing to do with what they've just said. Plus, you've just wasted a ton of energy anticipating what the person is going to say by filling in any blanks with thoughts of your own choosing instead of simply relaxing into the conversation and *hearing* what is said. Big difference.

INTERRUPT YOUR HABIT OF INTERRUPTING

I learned the simple solution to breaking the habit of interrupting while I was in London.

I was in a meeting with a group of strong executives who were very passionate about the topic being discussed. It seemed as if no one could talk for more than thirty seconds without being interrupted by someone else in the meeting. Everybody was competing to get their next thought added to the conversation.

The British are known for being polite, so each time one of them interrupted, they would say, "Sorry for interrupting," before launching into a monologue—which would inevitably get interrupted 30 seconds later by someone else with another "Sorry for interrupting."

And that's the solution to interrupting the habit of interrupting!

Apologize when you interrupt.

Apologizing when you interrupt brings more awareness to how frequently you do it. When we stop to apologize, it breaks the flow of the response and brings our awareness to the fact that we're, well, interrupting. Over time, you'll naturally do it less frequently. And even if you continue to interrupt, at least you'll be more polite about it and show others that you know you're doing it!

ASK FOR PERMISSION TO INTERRUPT

Our team in Europe was very multicultural. Every person spoke at least three languages. We would hold meetings in a mix of French, German, and English depending on who the client was. As the person who had the weakest language skills, I often found my mind wandering during conversations—I stopped listening, because I was lost. Because I didn't know the vocabulary, the jargon if you will, I would often get lost five minutes into an hour-long conversation. If I got lost at the beginning, it was like skipping to chapter 10 in a book. Without the context of the first five minutes, the remaining 55 minutes of the meeting was a waste of time.

Then I asked for permission to interrupt. "It's very difficult for me to follow and contribute because you are immersed in this language that's foreign to me. May I have your permission to interrupt if I don't understand something?"

Foreign language is everywhere in business, even if all of your meetings are in English. Have you ever been in a meeting with a bunch of accountants, engineers, or IT people? They have a language all their own. And what happens when you don't understand the language? You stop listening.

Sometimes, to listen more, you need to ask for permission to interrupt.

WHY YOU AREN'T LISTENING

Another reason that we don't listen is because we aren't interested in what the other person is saying.

What we say often affects whether others listen to what we say, but—more surprisingly—what we say directly affects whether others' responses will interest us. Instead of using our words to elevate the conversation, we're giving in to a response that reinforces our lack of interest or anticipation that we already know what comes next; therefore, why keep talking about it?

What if the reason people don't have anything interesting to say has everything to do with *your* words and little to do with *theirs*?

What if the secret to listening is *talking*?

In software engineering, we have a saying called *garbage in, garbage out*. It means a system is only as good as its inputs. Bad inputs yield bad outputs. As in manufacturing or cooking, if someone uses low-quality raw materials or low-quality ingredients, the finished product will reflect the same low quality.

Your questions are the inputs. If you ask questions that don't engage people, you'll get boring answers. Have some fun with it. Get more creative. Imagine a question that the other person isn't going to anticipate.

REPEAT WHAT THEY SAID, VERBATIM

Another eye-opening listening technique is adapted from the work of marriage expert Harville Hendrix. The exercise goes like this: one person speaks and the other person attempts to repeat their words, exactly. Try this. You'll discover two things. First, it's extremely difficult to repeat what someone said word-for-word if they speak for more than 20 seconds. Our memory can't store that much information. It will give you a new perspective on how often you speak without a pause—especially if you're speaking quickly because you're rushed, or excited about an idea. Consider the possibility that—rather than *saving* time—you are *wasting* your time by speaking so quickly. If the other person didn't hear what you said, was that an effective use of your time?

The second thing you'll discover—which is especially important in emotionally charged conversations—is that you hear things that the other person did not say. I would often find myself in conversations with my father where he would criticize me. "You're running the company into the ground!" he'd say. I'd fire back, "We grew 50 percent over the past three years and we were profitable; how is that running the company into the ground??!!"

When he said these things, what I heard was "You're doing a bad job." But my father *never* said those words. I heard what he didn't say. When he was saying "You're running the company into the ground!" what he was *really* saying is "I'm scared that a recession is coming and that our profit margins are too low to withstand a weak economy. I want you to increase profit margins."

When you get into emotionally charged conversations with a boss, coworker, spouse, or parent—what do you hear?

If you had a recording of what was actually said, does what you heard match the words they said?

Probably not.

ACKNOWLEDGE WHEN YOU'RE THINKING OF SOMETHING ELSE

Let's face it: there are many times when it's perfectly normal to not listen. Your mind will wander when other people are speaking. Or someone may come into your office and start talking while you're still thinking about a previous conversation or task. Research has shown that we are all terrible multitaskers, and the people who think they are great at multitasking are often the worst. Sometimes, you might stop listening to someone because something they say sparks an idea and you begin processing that idea as they continue to speak.

If you are face-to-face, then the other person probably knows when you're not listening—they can see it in your eyes. As with interrupting, if you find yourself not listening, just acknowledge it and apologize. Explain why you weren't listening and ask them to repeat themselves:

- I'm sorry. I wasn't listening.
- I was still thinking about the email I was writing before you walked in.
- Something you said sparked an idea, and I was thinking about it instead of listening to you.

By apologizing and acknowledging that you weren't listening, you will become more aware of how frequently you interrupt.

And one final tip for improving your listening. **Position yourself to face people when you speak with them. Do video calls instead of phone calls.** Whether you're talking to your spouse over dinner, tucking your children into bed, or calling someone halfway around the world, make sure the other person can see your eyes. When you know someone can see your eyes, it will help you resist distractions and help them to see that you are listening.

As you ask better questions and listen to the answers, you'll start a shift where people around you will feel more like partners.

PART 3

—

THE PARTNER
SHIFTS

**Tools to Build Better Partners—
and Become One**

Ten statements that make you a better partner, parent, and boss.

Take the Leader's Creed Challenge.

The Talk*SHIFTs* blend real-world business tools and multilingual leadership insights with research-based communication techniques. Talk*SHIFTs* use business best practices not only to create great teams, but—here's the bonus—they also create great families. Everyone has the opportunity to be a leader—some lead teams, others lead families—and we all have an opportunity to influence our friends, peers, and communities by setting an inspiring example.

There is a tool I developed that I've now introduced to thousands of leaders in my keynotes. Leaders report that using this tool is often a turning point in their relationship with someone. It's called the Leader's Creed Challenge.

This challenge is very simple, but, as you'll see in a moment, it's *not* easy. For many, it's extremely uncomfortable. That's why it's called the Leader's Creed *Challenge*.

You'll need a partner.

A partner is someone about whom you would *strongly agree* with the following statement: *it is very important to me that this person is engaged and committed one year from now.*

Write down the names of the people on your "team" who you *really* want to be engaged and committed one year from now.

Who would you add to this list if you expanded the definition of your "team" to include anyone who is an important part of your *life*? I suspect that you'd like your family members to be engaged and committed members of your "team" too, right?

Congratulations, you've completed the first step to the Leader's Creed Challenge!

The first time I did a live test-drive of the Leader's Creed Challenge with a partner, the partner I chose was not a team member from work.

That partner was my seven-year-old son. It was Father's Day.

When I created the first version of the Leader's Creed Challenge, I recall thinking, "Why is it that most parents would say they love their children, but not all children feel loved?"

What if we could look at the specific behaviors that make up a good relationship, then ask a partner how they think we are doing with those behaviors?

Whether you think you are a good leader of a family, a business, or even a team is irrelevant. The only question that matters is this: do you have a good relationship *in the eyes of your partners*?

Men—myself included—are more likely to be unaware of serious problems in their personal and professional relationships. That's one reason why twice as many women as men file for divorce, and in marriages where the wife is college-educated, women initiate the divorce 90 percent of the time. And according to the world's top researcher into marriage and divorce, Dr. John Gottman, *the primary predictor of marital satisfaction is the man's behavior.*[10] You could say the same about employee satisfaction by substituting "boss" for man. You're probably aware of the old saying "People don't leave jobs; they leave bosses."

That's why the Leader's Creed Challenge is powerful in family relationships as well as in work relationships or any partnership that is important to you. If you're not comfortable doing the Leader's Creed Challenge at work, try it with your spouse or partner at home. If you're not comfortable taking the challenge with your spouse, try it with someone at work, a child, a parent, or a close friend.

You'll notice that nine of the ten statements are exactly the same, regardless of whether you are speaking the Leader's Creed to your spouse, your child, or someone on your team.

THE FIRST NINE STATEMENTS
OF THE LEADER'S CREED

1. I demonstrate kindness and respect toward you in ways that you can see and hear.

2. I listen when you speak.

3. I am aware when I hurt you, and I apologize when I do.

4. I show interest in your career and development as a person.

5. I demonstrate how to respectfully request changes in the behavior of others, including my requests of you.

6. With my words and actions, I build you up rather than tear you down.

7. I effectively communicate my emotions and needs and create a safe place for you to communicate yours.

8. I express anger appropriately.

9. I surround us with people who enhance our lives, and distance us from people who don't.

We are always improving the Leader's Creed based upon reader feedback and experience, so we recommend you download the latest version of the worksheet at **www.TheLeadersCreed.com**.

The first time I did the Leader's Creed Challenge, I grabbed a pen and introduced the idea to my seven-year-old son while tucking him into bed.

You can use these words as a basis for introducing the Leader's Creed Challenge to someone in your life.

"Hey buddy, I want to be a great dad. To help me to be the best dad I can be, I have some questions that I'd like to ask you. Are you ready?"

He hesitated, then said, "Okay."

"It's really important to me that you're honest and tell me what you really think. I want to know what I can do to be better, okay? You know you can always tell me anything, right?"

"Yes, Dad."

"Okay. Here's how it works. I am going to read a sentence, then I am going to ask you: on a scale of 1 to 10, how strongly do you agree with that statement? Ten is completely agree and one is totally disagree.

"Here's the first sentence.

"I listen when you speak."

I paused for about five seconds to let him think about it, then asked, "On a scale of 1 to 10, how strongly do you agree with that statement?"

"Six," he said.

"Six?!" I looked at him sideways, raising an eyebrow. "SIX!!! SIX!!!" I laughed and tickled him.

"I really appreciate you being honest, buddy. I can imagine it takes some courage to say six. I really appreciate it. So, I've got another question for you. What would be the difference between a six and a nine? What would you suggest that I start doing, or stop doing?"

"Well, you do look at your phone a lot when I'm talking," he said.

"You're right. I do look at my phone a lot. Here's what I'm going to do. I am going to put my phone in the bedroom from six to eight o'clock every night. I'm going to write down your responses and what I'm committed to doing differently so that we can look at how we improve every year on Father's Day. Is that okay with you?"

While he watched, I spoke aloud what I wrote on the worksheet: "Six. I will put my phone in bedroom every night from six to eight o'clock.

"Now, sometimes I look at my phone and I don't even realize it. Would you be open to helping me out? If I'm looking at my phone instead of listening to you, you have my permission to say, 'Dad, you're looking at your phone again!' It might be uncomfortable to tell me that, especially if other people are around. So maybe we have a secret code word. If you could pick a funny code word, what would you choose?"

"Purple elephant," he responded.

"Okay, in the future, if you say 'purple elephant,' then I will hear 'Dad, you're looking at your phone.'"

I wrote *purple elephant code word* on the worksheet.

We continued through the ten statements of the Father's Creed. What I found most useful was taking notes of exactly what he said using his own words, and the actions that I committed to taking, so that we could review them together the following year.

"Okay, buddy, we're almost at the end. Here's that last one," I said.

"I demonstrate love, kindness, and respect toward your mother with my words and actions, even when she is not around. What would you say about that one, on a scale of one to ten?"

"Nine," he said.

That was one of the proudest moments since my divorce. How you treat the mother (or father) of your children will become the unconscious baseline of what your children will expect—and accept—in their romantic relationships. Married or divorced, the parameters of your relationship will become the default setting for your kids.

THE TENTH STATEMENT OF
THE LEADER'S CREED

The tenth statement is slightly different depending on whether you are reading the Leader's Creed to someone who works for you (the Leader's Creed), to your spouse (the Couple's Creed), or to your child (the Father's Creed and the Mother's Creed).

The Leader's Creed: With my words and actions, I demonstrate kindness and respect toward *coworkers, customers, and business partners*, even when they are not around.

The Couple's Creed: With my words and actions, I demonstrate love, kindness, and respect toward *our family members*, even when they are not around.

The Father's Creed: With my words and actions, I demonstrate love, kindness, and respect toward *your mother*, even when she is not around.*

The Mother's Creed: With my words and actions, I demonstrate love, kindness, and respect toward *your father*, even when he is not around.*

* Note that this statement applies even if you are not married to the mother or father of your child. In fact, showing leadership in this area is not only more difficult, but it is also *more important* to the emotional development of your child.

THE LEADER'S CREED AT WORK

While the story above illustrates how to do the challenge with a family member, the process is pretty much the same with a team member at work.

The reason the Leader's Creed Challenge is so powerful is that these statements are in the present tense, and you are making concrete commitments to your partner during the challenge. (We'll explore the language of how to make commitments that stick later in Talk*SHIFT* #21: Actions Don't Speak, Words Do.)

It's very important to use the wording of the Leader's Creed exactly. There is a very important difference between asking someone whether they agree with the statement *I listen when you speak* compared to *I have good listening skills*. If I disagree that you have good listening skills, it's easier for you to rationalize away my judgment of your listening skills. Or maybe I will say that you have good listening skills—I've seen you listen to others—but you don't listen to *me*. And ultimately, whether someone has the *ability* to listen is irrelevant if they don't listen to *you*, right?

These subtle wording differences are the reason why the Leader's Creed and the Talk*SHIFT* Assessment can complement traditional 360s and catalyze a deeper desire in people to change.

To avoid the end, avoid the beginning of the end.

The secret to long-term partnerships is this: to stop people from leaving your organization, stop them from looking.

You may logically think that you lose your best talent when they march into your office and tell you they've been made a better offer. This scenario applies to your top performers, your spouse (even if their better offer is the choice to be without you), or a valued partnership of any kind. You may think that in this scenario you now are in a fight to "win" them back by bettering their fabulous new job offer, offering to spend more time at home and wash the dishes every night, or stepping up on any demand a partner needs to be more satisfied. But you began losing them long ago.

That moment can spark from many origins. It can be when they realized that they aren't appreciated or acknowledged for their contribution. It can be a dramatic and hurtful event such as being passed over for a promotion or being criticized once too often. The list of what employees value can be extremely broad, and companies are spending large amounts to assess engagement, autonomy needs, recognition, compensation, and physical work environment. Spouses are sinking dollars into therapy and counseling, working to repair wounds created months or years before.

This Talk*SHIFT* isn't about the collective forces that lure your top talent away or inspire your spouse to change the lock on the door. This Talk*SHIFT* is about the moments that matter.

Great leaders don't stop people from *leaving*, they stop people from wanting to look. The end begins in that moment when your top talent, spouse, or any partner first thinks of leaving (for another job, a separation, a business breakup). To avoid losing key partners, avoid the beginning of the end.

This is a good time to be reminded of the Pareto principle, also called the 80/20 rule, which states that in most teams and organizations the top 20 percent of the people deliver 80 percent of the results. This is where your efforts to retain talent need to be placed. True, there is associated cost with every employee lost, but the high engagement of these top performers is key to the success of every organization.

The moment you lose is the moment when the thought of leaving enters the mind of your best talent. That moment is the beginning of the end.

Recruiters are going to keep coming for them, and you can count on that. In the days before LinkedIn, there was a lot more effort associated with starting to look for a new job. An employee had to create a résumé. Then search job boards and apply for jobs. By some estimates, over 85 percent of the American workforce has a profile on LinkedIn.[11] For many, a LinkedIn profile eliminates the need to prepare a formal résumé in order to receive unsolicited emails from recruiters. Your best people are frequently receiving emails from recruiters—especially in high-demand sectors like sales or IT. For the process of leaving to begin, all it takes is one bad moment on the day that one of these inquiries lands in their inbox. They might be thinking, "Maybe today is the day that I will start paying attention to the emails from recruiters that are landing in my LinkedIn inbox."

Are you willing to risk that today is the day that they start looking?

What do you do that starts people thinking about looking?

Ask them with this TalkSHIFT:

"It's really important to me that you enjoy your work here. On the days that you find yourself most frustrated, what has happened? What do we need to start doing, or stop doing, that would reduce or eliminate your frustration?"

This can be a difficult question to ask. But it's worth it.

What's the cost of a breakup? If you add up the legal costs, incremental expenses, lost revenues, and profits over the next five years, what would be the cost of a breakup with your best employee? Your business partner? Your top salesperson? Your most important executive? Your most knowledgeable customer service person? Or the brilliant R & D person who drives innovation in your company?

Getting closer to home, what would be the cost of a breakup with your spouse? My lawyer friends say the odds are that it will be 50 percent of your net worth. But 50 percent of your net worth is just the *baseline* cost of a breakup.

After my divorce, I did a lot of dating before settling down with my current partner. I'm not one for light conversation, so I would often ask, "Tell me about the first moment you decided to leave your marriage."

In every case, the woman immediately shared a moment that the thought of leaving began. In most cases, it was years before she actually said the words "I want a divorce." And the research supports this. Over half of partners who initiate a divorce have been thinking about it for over a year before they finally take action.

I started asking executives the same question: "Tell me about the first moment you decided to leave your former job." They could immediately recall a moment that started the thought process. Sometimes the leaving was swift; other times it took longer, but the interest in leaving was activated.

THE REVERSE *SHIFT*

Well, it would be great if the people around us behaved in a way that stopped our desire to look, but what can we do to stop *ourselves* from looking?

Too often, the moment we decide to leave is an emotional reaction. Someone says or does something that triggers us to think, "I'm out!" In that moment, we mentally check out of the job (or the relationship), even though it may be months or years before we finally leave. Rather than checking out, the shift is to commit in that moment to having a conversation with the person who has the power to change the circumstances (or behaviors) that result in your decision to leave. You can do it with this shift:

> When [*insert the event that caused you to decide to leave*], my initial gut reaction was that this was the last straw, and I decided to leave. Rather than keeping you in the dark as I planned my exit, I committed to having the courage to speak to you about it to see if there is a way forward.

You are not recommitting to the relationship here; you are simply committing to step into a courageous conversation that may be a catalyst for you to recommit.

The people who take control of their happiness are the ones who regularly ask themselves:

> Instead of investing time to find a new job (or relationship), how can I invest in this one to make it better?

Too often, people conclude that there is no amount of investment that will make the current one better because we believe that our boss or our partner is the problem.

Many people believe that if your heart is in the right place, then the right words will automatically follow. It's a nice thought, but in my experience, that's simply not true. I have met my fair share of toxic leaders in corner offices around the globe, but I have never met a leader who wakes up in the morning, looks at themselves in the bathroom mirror, and says, "I think I'm going to be a jerk today!" Most leaders— even "toxic" ones—believe their hearts are in the right place.

While the other 21 Talk*SHIFTs* in this book give you many ways to rethink what you say, this particular one serves as a reminder that moments count and that you can win or begin to lose in any moment.

I don't mention this to set up a virtual minefield—I tell you this because if you are unaware of when you begin to lose your best talent and partnerships, you are going to lose them.

You will make mistakes. We all do. To safeguard our working and personal relationships from these little mistakes requires emotional connection.

Speak like an emotional Einstein using the language of empathy.

To develop emotional intelligence and
increase connection, use these words.

Once upon a time, I was an emotional Einstein. An "emotional Einstein" is someone who *intellectually* understands emotional intelligence, but is unknowingly speaking thoughts instead of emotions. I'd read countless books on emotional intelligence. Yet none of these books touched on the subtle—but critical—changes to our words that are the difference between analytical communication that disconnects us and emotional communication that connects us.

I'm not alone. Emotional intelligence has been around for over 20 years. You'd be hard-pressed to find a senior executive who doesn't know about emotional intelligence (which is why I won't review it here). And yet, twenty years later, emotional Einsteins are everywhere in business.

Creating emotional connection takes time. Many of us are uncomfortable expressing emotion, especially at work. Shying away from the work to create emotional connection is another form of lazy leadership. The Talk*SHIFTs* in this chapter are simple, practical language tools to help you identify and communicate *your* emotions, as well as to help others to identify and communicate *their* emotions.

Over 20 years after it was invented, emotional intelligence is still a common leadership topic. Why? Because lack of emotional intelligence is still a problem in the workplace. And why is that? It is nearly impossible to improve our emotional intelligence without a language for identifying and communicating emotion.

IDENTIFYING EMOTIONS IN OURSELVES AND OTHERS

Imagine the last time you asked someone "How are you feeling?"

Do you remember what they said? I suspect it was "I'm feeling fine" or "I'm okay" or "I feel great." The problem here is that the words *fine*, *okay*, and *great* are not feelings. They are not emotions. These words do not create emotional connection.

A simple upgrade is to replace the word *how* with *what*. If you ask "What are you feeling?" it's more difficult for people to respond with *fine*, *okay*, or *great*. (Some people will still do this out of habit.)

If you see a flash of emotion on someone's face, an even more powerful way to ask is "What emotion are you experiencing right now?" or simply "What are you feeling right now?" Alternatively, if someone is telling you a story of something emotional that happened in the past, ask "What emotion *were* you experiencing in that moment?"

This tool is equally useful for identifying our own emotions. If you develop a habit of becoming more aware of your own emotions by asking "What am I feeling right now?" you'll find that you'll be more likely to change the words you use when talking with others.

As you begin to ask yourself and others to identify their emotions, you'll find that many people have a hard time finding the right words for the emotion they're experiencing. When we don't know the emotion we're experiencing, "I feel fine" is an easy way to avoid the question.

To identify the emotion, it's useful to ask the following multiple-choice question: "If forced to choose from the following emotions, which one comes closest: happiness, love, anger, fear, sadness, shame, disgust, or surprise?"

The emotions above are the primary families of emotions. Since the days of Aristotle, philosophers, and more recently psychologists, have classified emotions into core emotions or families of emotions. Think of families of emotions as branches on a tree. For example, there's a major branch on the tree for *anger*. The branch splits off into various smaller branches that may include *rage* (an intense form of anger) and milder forms of *anger* like *annoyance, disappointment,* or *frustration.*

After we identify the emotion family, we can further refine by asking something like "Within the category of anger, which of the following comes closest: rage, annoyance, or frustration?"

HOW ENGLISH GETS IN THE WAY OF COMMUNICATING EMOTION

English speakers have a unique challenge when expressing emotion because English gets in the way of expressing emotions in a way that many other languages do not. If you look up the word *feel* in an English thesaurus, you will discover that the word *think* is a synonym. But if you look up the French word for *feel, sentir,* in a thesaurus, you won't find the French word for *think, penser,* as a synonym. It's the same for German and many other languages.

As a result, we sometimes fool ourselves into thinking we are speaking in an emotionally intelligent way when we are not. Despite reading countless books on emotional intelligence, I fooled myself this way for nearly 20 years.

Here's what it looks like:

- I feel like I've been hit by a bus.
- I feel that you did that on purpose.

The statements above are not feelings. They are *thoughts*. I do not *feel* that you did that on purpose. I *think* that you did that on purpose. When you express thoughts, especially in emotionally charged moments, your words often lead to disconnection.

Here's the solution. Eliminate the word *like* or *that* after the word *feel*. The next word after *feel* should always be an emotion word:

I feel [*emotion word*]:

- I feel sad.
- I feel angry.

In some teams and corporate cultures, you may be uncomfortable saying *I feel*. If so, you can replace *I feel [emotion word]* with *I am [emotion word]*. For example, *I feel sad* becomes *I am sad*. *I felt angry* becomes *I was angry*.

THE LANGUAGE OF EMPATHY

You'll recall that in Talk*SHIFT* #6 we introduced Dr. Marshall Rosenberg's work.

Empathy guesses were one of Dr. Rosenberg's greatest innovations. Empathy guesses can be especially useful for analytical people who struggle with developing emotional intelligence.

You can use empathy guesses to shift a conversation to a deeper level about the underlying emotions that the other person is experiencing. Dr. Rosenberg's language for empathy guesses is this:

- **I'm guessing** that you're feeling [*emotion word*].
- **I'm guessing** that you're feeling *afraid*.

In the business world, some may perceive you as uncertain or weak if you use the words *guess* and *feeling*. For this reason, in business, I'd recommend replacing the word *guess* with one the following:

- **I wonder** if you're [*emotion word*]. **I sense** that you might be [*emotion word*] about this.
- **I wonder** if you're *afraid*. **I sense** that you might be *anxious* about this.

Here's the brilliant thing about empathy guesses: you don't have to guess correctly to develop your emotional intelligence and begin attuning to the other person! When you make empathy guesses, according to Dr. Rosenberg, people will often correct you if you guess incorrectly. The implication of this is that anyone, at any level of emotional intelligence, can become more emotionally attuned through a process of trial and error. As you make more empathy guesses with a specific person and they correct you, you will begin to get a better sense of that person. Because people tend to react in similar ways across cultures, not only do you get a better sense of that individual, but you will get a better sense of people in general.

BEWARE FALSE FEELINGS

There are many emotion words that are not helpful because they imply that the other person has done something *to* us. These "false feeling" words place blame for our emotional state onto someone else. These emotions are often judgments of something the other has done *to* us. False feelings are almost always associated with words that end in the letters -*ed*, such as the false feeling *betrayed*. In a sensitive conversation, saying "I feel frustrated" will often cause the other person to hear "You frustrated me." The actual emotion here is *frustration*.

False feelings do not fit well into the following sentence based upon the question we used to identify emotion:

The emotion I am experiencing right now is *frustrated*.

There's an easy way to identify these false feelings. They almost always complete the sentence *You _____ me,* as in *You disappointed me. You disappointed me* makes a logical sentence, but *You sadness me* does not. *Sadness* is a feeling, *disappointed* is an action—and in this case it's a judgmental action that typically causes the person who hears it to become afraid or defensive.

Many of these words are not emotions at all, but some give

us clues to the emotion. Disappointment and frustration are emotions. Imagine you're in an emotionally charged conversation with someone who is angry with you and they say, "The emotion I'm experiencing is frustration." Compare that with "I'm feeling frustrated." It's a subtle difference.

Anger and false feelings typically go hand in hand. Here are more examples of false emotions: abandoned, abused, attacked, betrayed, bullied, cheated, diminished, intimidated, let down, manipulated, misunderstood, neglected, overworked, pressured, rejected, taken for granted, threatened, unappreciated, unheard, unsupported, unwanted, used.

Whenever you hear these false feelings, consider them a signal for anger.

How we communicate our anger—and respond to anger from others—is critical to maintaining strong, lasting partnerships.

The iceberg of anger conceals the keys to connection.

Discover the emotions beneath anger in yourself and others, and connect on the emotions you find.

Anger rarely increases connection, but it can destroy it in an instant. Long term, it can impede a growing connection because there is still a lingering memory of a moment of anger. Let's face it: few of us want to be around angry people and fewer want to have any form of anger directed at us. There are words we can use to shift anger—our own anger and the anger of others—and cultivate compassion and connection instead.

From this moment forward, whenever you see, hear, or experience anger, say to yourself: "In anger is an opportunity for connection." If you are angry with someone, you have an opportunity for connection. If someone else is angry with you, consider it an opportunity for connection. Even if someone comes to you and they're angry with *someone else*, there's both an opportunity for you to increase your connection with the person who's angry and an opportunity for them to create connection with the person with whom they're angry.

THE DIFFERENCE WITH ANGER

Anger is different from the other emotions. Psychologists often refer to anger as a *secondary* emotion because it is a signal of one of the primary emotions: fear, shame, guilt, hurt, or sadness.

Primary emotions create connection. Anger erodes connection. Yet anger can become the gateway to connection if we get in touch with the emotion behind the anger. Rather than expressing anger, if we can identify and then express the emotion beneath our anger, we can shift from anger to deeper emotions that connect us.

Think about it the last time you were really angry.

What emotion was beneath your anger? Was it fear? Did someone hurt you? Were you embarrassed (a milder form of shame)? Often, we feel *guilty* or *ashamed* about something that *we* have done, but it shows up as anger toward *others*. Is there something that you are guilty or ashamed about, yet you express your guilt as anger toward a family member or coworker? When this happens, you'll often find that you express your anger toward the very person who you have hurt.

ANGER AT WORK

In my experience, the most common emotion for leaders is anger (or its milder sibling, *frustration*). Interestingly, the frustration leaders experience is frequently because their perception of the job is different than the actual job. This is very common for entrepreneurs and leaders who once did the job of those who frustrate them. Those leaders often played that role or a similar role when the company—or team—was smaller. Years later, the team has grown to ten times the size, and the job is much more complex. Leaders project the way the job was when they were starting out onto the team and wonder "Why is this taking so long?!"

And so, leaders get frustrated with employees who complete tasks late or incorrectly.

What happens next when the boss is angry?

The boss often expresses their anger in some way. (Hopefully a healthy way.) A healthy way for a boss to express anger would be to have a conversation with the employee.

Imagine your boss says to you, "I'm angry because you haven't solved this problem."

What emotion do you experience when your boss is angry?

Fear.

When you are afraid, research shows that the part of your

brain responsible for creativity shuts down. If the part of your brain responsible for creativity isn't working, how likely is it that you will come up with your best ideas to solve the problem?

When you express your anger with someone who reports to you, you're making it less likely that they will solve the problem!

What's the solution?

Before you share your anger with someone, ask yourself:

Which of the following emotions is behind my anger: sadness, hurt, guilt, shame, or fear?

Remember, anger is an opportunity to connect. Primary emotions connect. Anger disconnects.

Once you've identified the deeper emotion beneath your anger, share that emotion: fear, hurt, shame (embarrassment), or sadness. If someone who you care about comes to you and says "I'm hurt" or "I'm afraid," isn't your natural reaction to help them? When you are in a state of fear, your creative brain is unavailable to find solutions that can help!

> Replace this: I'm *angry* because the project is late.
> With: I'm *afraid* because this project is late.

Then follow up with the reason why you are afraid:

I'm afraid because our team could lose our bonus if we lose this customer.

There's one case where the above won't work. What if the person wants your team to lose their bonus? What if they don't like you? What if the person is purposely doing something (possibly in a passive-aggressive way) to hurt you or cause you to be afraid?

If that is the case, there is a larger shift needed, because your relationship is broken and a change in words alone won't create connection. We will explore powerful tools to repair broken relationships in Talk*SHIFT* #22 *Say sorry less. Apologize more.*

*SHIFT*ING FROM ANGER TO COMPASSION

When I first met her, Amy was a divorced executive with three young children. She was in a contentious co-parenting partnership with her former spouse. (If you have children, ex-spouses continue to be your parenting partner.) Her ex-spouse's inflexibility on custody schedules was impacting her ability to travel for work. Her ex-spouse was unemployed. Amy was required to pay a large alimony for 15 years following their divorce, despite the fact that it was his infidelity that ultimately broke up their marriage. Twelve years after the divorce, his behavior was getting more aggressive. Every couple of weeks, he would leave derogatory voice-mail messages or send aggressive texts. Often, these exchanges came shortly after her alimony check arrived in the mail. She had plenty of reasons to be angry.

The turning point for Amy began by asking herself the following question:

Which of the following is behind my ex-husband's anger: sadness, hurt, guilt, shame, or fear?

"Fear," she told herself. "He's afraid that he can't afford his house when the alimony stops. He's afraid he won't find another relationship."

And then she asked herself the follow-up question: what about guilt, sadness, or shame?

She knew the answer. "Yes, shame and guilt. While he will never say it, he knows that it was his behavior that ultimately caused me to leave. He's ashamed that he is reliant on his ex-wife for financial support."

These questions shifted Amy's anger toward compassion for him. She began asking herself the question above before she responded to any nasty messages from her ex. In doing so, she shifted her own anger toward compassion and reminded herself, "He's afraid, ashamed, and guilty." When she responded to him from that frame of mind, she was able to shift her anger. Within three months, their co-parenting partnership improved dramatically, he became more flexible around custody, and the aggressive text messages stopped.

Amy suspects that her ex-husband was angry at himself, but he was redirecting that anger at her. Understanding this gave her better ways of both coping and working toward better solutions with her ex-husband.

While this example is from a wound in a fractured marriage, leaders are just as apt to redirect anger toward themselves at their subordinates.

Sometimes the most destructive anger is the anger we feel toward ourselves. Are you angry with yourself? That is why it's so important to become aware of the words we speak to ourselves.

The words we speak to others echo the words we speak to ourselves.

Self-talk lessons from an aikido dojo

We often don't realize the far-reaching impact of the words we use in the office. I learned how far a leader's words echo—and for how long they echo—in an unlikely place: a workshop in an Aikido dojo outside of San Francisco.

The leader separated the group into pairs and introduced us to an exercise he called "The Grab."

I was partnered with an attractive woman, so, a bit nervous, I tried to break the ice by saying, "I bet the legal people don't recommend 'The Grab' in the office." Dead silence.

The leader continued, "This exercise is meant to teach us

how to make requests of people. Think of a request that you would like to make of someone. Imagine your partner is that person. Then walk up to the person, grab them by the arm, and make your request."

I thought, "This is just weird. I've been leading and telling people what to do for twenty years! What could I possibly learn from this exercise?"

The leader looked straight at me and, as if reading my mind, added, "If you feel like making requests of others isn't an area you need to work on, imagine that the person you're making a request of is *yourself*. Is there a request you frequently make of yourself that you don't comply with?"

I thought, "Well, I'm always struggling to get myself to work out. I'll try that."

My partner held out her arm. The instructor said, "Take three steps back, walk up to your partner, and grab them by the arm somewhat forcefully. Make your request, then ask them what came to their mind."

I had never really thought about the words I use to make myself get up off the couch to go work out. I considered it for a moment.

Finally, I walked up, gingerly grabbed her outstretched arm, and said in a fairly stern tone, "You're undisciplined and lazy. You should go work out." She stared at me with no discernable facial expression.

I stepped back and asked her what she was thinking.

"I didn't want to do it," she said rapidly. "In fact, I wanted to rebel against you and do the opposite!" She paused and then said, "Maybe try it again, but this time speak to me like I'm an eight-year-old boy. Speak to me like you would your own son."

I stepped back and tried again.

"Hey, buddy, let's go work out! You know what? After we do, we'll feel great and have more energy for the rest of the day!"

My partner said, "It made me really want to go work out when you said it that way!"

How do *you* speak to yourself?

How often do you admonish yourself and engage in negative self-talk when you resist doing things that are good for you? Do you consider the way in which you talk to yourself to be kind? Or inspirational?

The words we speak to others echo the words we speak to ourselves.

This Talk*SHIFT* is about changing the words you say to yourself. But where do the words we speak to others come from? Usually, they come from the people who we admire or those whose approval we seek. Our leaders.

Who are our real first leaders? After the exercise at the dojo,

I asked myself, "Why would I call myself *undisciplined and lazy*?" Where did the words *undisciplined and lazy* come from?

They came from my father.

When I was twelve years old, my father frequently called me "undisciplined and lazy." Years later, despite twenty years of working sixty- to ninety-hour work weeks, I still sometimes catch myself in self-talk telling myself that I am "undisciplined and lazy."

At nineteen, I was an intern at IBM when CEO Lou Gerstner joined to save the company. At the bottom of a sprawling global company with over 100,000 employees, I was more than ten layers of management away from the CEO. Five days after Gerstner joined, we had our first department meeting. My manager spoke differently that day than he ever had before.

"I don't have PowerPoint slides today. We are just going to talk," he said.

It took only *five days* for the language of the new CEO to ripple through ten layers of management to the hundreds of thousands of IBM employees.

You've likely noticed this rapid shift in language when a friend or spouse changes jobs or gets a new boss. Maybe the new leader prefers to "touch base" instead of "have a meeting," and suddenly your friend or spouse is using the phrase "touching base" in their personal lives. Maybe your spouse says, "We need to touch base after dinner, so we can talk about our plans for the weekend."

Parents are leaders of the family in the same way that bosses and executives lead our companies. Be mindful of the words you use with your children and spouse, because your words will echo through the communication patterns in their minds and your family for decades to come. How often do you find yourself saying, "My mom used to say that" or have the realization that you're repeating a negative language pattern that your parent used, such as "You'll never get a decent job if you (get a tattoo, fail math, fill in the blank)."

Along with all of the positive efforts we now make to help employees and our families enjoy life, build confidence, and stay motivated, the words we speak have a tremendous effect. One negative or thoughtless remark can immediately create a chasm between effort and result. What words are you using with your children that will echo in their minds for decades to come?

To learn new language patterns, including terms, phrases, and verbal expressions, try out some new choices and observe for response. Start with talking to yourself in a new way and notice what works.

Then, practice it everywhere. Practice the Talk*SHIFT* with *everyone* in your life—not only your boss, your team, and your customers but also your spouse, your children, and your family members. Notice their reaction and resulting actions.

THE SELF-TALK*SHIFT*

When was the last time you said to yourself that you were going to do something, but you didn't do it? Perhaps you posted a to-do list or simply made a mental note. Maybe it was something positive, like "I'm going to work out tomorrow" or "I am going to get up early."

The next time you don't follow up, tune into how you talk to yourself. What are the exact words that you say to yourself? Write these words down. Now, rewrite these in words that you would use if you were encouraging an eight-year-old. Imagine the tone of voice you would use when you're encouraging an eight-year-old to do something that they clearly don't want to do. Use those same words with yourself the next time.

For me, it's "Hey buddy, let's go work out. We're going to have so much energy and fun."

When you address yourself, address yourself as "we" instead of "I." Rather than "I should go work out," say "Let's work out. When we work out, we'll feel great and have so much energy for the day."

This seems like a workaround, but it works. It may seem embarrassing to talk to yourself this way, but who else will know? You've partnered with yourself!

EXTENDING YOUR SELF-TALK TO OTHERS

As you make the effort to use more positive words, more actionable phrases, and a lively and upbeat tone, really stop yourself and redirect when you hear anything that doesn't fit with your intention. What words are you committed to *stop* speaking to your children or your spouse? *Practice* alternatives.

Keep the echo going with words you and others will want to hear!

Actions don't speak. Words do.

Flip the old cliché that actions speaker louder than words. Use these words to make commitments that are followed with action.

October 21, 1997, 8:30 p.m. St. Louis time (9:30 a.m. Hong Kong time)—my first conversation with a Chinese executive. I'm 24 years old, on the telephone with Mr. Wong.

In his thick Chinese accent, he says, "Krister, I want the specification document by Friday. It must be two hundred pages at least."

I respond, "Okay. I will get it to you Friday."

As I hang up, a smile comes to my face and I think, "Friday at 5 p.m. St. Louis time is 6 a.m. Hong Kong time, but Mr. Wong doesn't check email on weekends, so I have until Monday at 9 a.m. Hong Kong time, which is 7 p.m. Sunday night."

Needless to say, Mr. Wong was not amused on Monday at 9 a.m. He had planned to read the document over the weekend.

✶ ✶ ✶

"Actions speak louder than words," we tell ourselves when someone says they will do something repeatedly but their actions don't match their words.

The words we use when we make commitments to ourselves and others set the stage for the action that will follow, and our word choices can have a significant impact on whether our actions will match our words. By walking our own talk and modeling this behavior, we can increase the congruence between the commitments and actions of those around us too.

As we follow through on the commitments that we make to ourselves and others, we respect ourselves more. Conversely, we lose respect for people who do not follow through on their commitments. This includes losing respect for ourselves for those private commitments we make. Delivering on the private commitments we make to ourselves, like "I'm going to the gym in the morning" or "I'm going to get to work early tomorrow" builds our self-esteem.

When you make commitments to others following the rules below, you'll find that people are more likely to believe that you will follow through on your commitments.

REMOVE CONDITIONS OR UNCERTAINTY

As Yoda says, "Do or do not. There is no try." Eliminate the word *try*. Compare "I will *try to arrive* at work early tomorrow" to "I will *arrive* at work early tomorrow."

Similarly, watch out for the difference between using the words *if* and *when*. This is especially important in our self-talk. Compare "I will reward myself with new clothes *if* I lose ten pounds" to "I will reward myself with new clothes *when* I lose ten pounds." (Interesting side note: the German word for *if* is *wenn*, which is pronounced exactly like the word *when*. This can create some interesting confusion when speaking English with Germans!)

BE SPECIFIC

How much earlier will you arrive to work? Two minutes earlier or 30 minutes earlier? As we make our commitments specific, we ensure more certainty and remove the temptation to create our own wiggle room.

Being clear with time commitments, especially when there are varying time zones, can make a big difference in customer satisfaction (and with bosses too).

Specificity also helps with commitments we make to others. Imagine telling your boss or spouse, "I will finish it next week." Because we are ambiguous with our time commitment, we can actually increase anxiety and potential for loss of trust and respect from others. Your spouse thinks that "next week" means Monday, or at the very latest Friday. When you finish on Sunday, within your understanding of the week, your spouse is more likely to be disappointed.

Even more, without specificity, you may be setting up an environment with the potential for conflict and frustration for yourself. If your boss asks on Wednesday when you'll be finished, you may say to yourself, "I told him next week! My boss is a micromanager!"

Compare "I will finish it next week" to "I will finish before 12 p.m. on Wednesday." Now if your boss sends you an email at 1 p.m. on Wednesday, it's perfectly understandable, because you are outside of the bounds of your commitment.

And specificity applies to a lot more than just time. In the above example, consider what *finish* means. Imagine the task you are committing to is a written document, like a report. Will you send a draft or the final version by 12 p.m. on Wednesday? Will it be a one-page report or a fifty-page report? While you may not know all of the details when you make a commitment, using specifics ties you more firmly to your intention of action.

SPEAK YOUR COMMITMENT TO OTHERS

If we tell others about our commitments, we are more likely to follow through because of what psychologists call cognitive dissonance. Cognitive dissonance is the experience of psychological stress that occurs when a person holds two or more contradictory beliefs, ideas, or values, or participates in an action that goes against one of these three.[12]

The more people we tell about something, the more our self-esteem will be reinforced when we follow through, thus increasing the accountability that we place upon ourselves. Imagine this thought experiment. You want to lose 30 pounds. Imagine buying Facebook and LinkedIn ads where—every day—your friends and business connections will see a picture of you under the headline "I WILL LOSE 30 POUNDS BY MARCH 1st." (For what it's worth, you can actually do this for less than the price of your gym membership!) Wouldn't that be a powerful motivator? Imagine that every time you see your friends, they ask, "How is your weight loss goal going?" After a couple days, they won't even need to ask, because you'll know that's what they are thinking.

PRE-COMMIT TO ACCOUNTABILITY

Another powerful tool is to pre-commit to what will you do if you miss your commitment. For example, "If I don't finish by 12 p.m. Wednesday, I will send you an email revising my committed date and time and explaining the reason why I missed my commitment." This eliminates the frustration for the other person if you do not meet your commitment. They aren't left asking themselves when a good time might be to follow up with you. If the person is able to rely on your commitment to reset the new date, this also eliminates the need for them to keep a running list of your commitments with your due dates. Your boss will love you if you do this consistently!

Your boss will love you even more if you take the pre-commitment even further. What if your boss planned time to review your report at 12 p.m. on Wednesday? Or your spouse made some plans that were contingent on your meeting your commitment? They are likely to be disappointed when they get an email at 12 p.m. on Wednesday, right?

To take your pre-commitment even further, consider making the following commitment: "If something changes that impacts my ability to meet my 12 p.m. Wednesday commitment to you, I will let you know as soon as I know."

WRITE IT DOWN AND READ IT ALOUD

As you make commitments to others, write those commitments down. If possible, allow the other person to see that you are writing down your commitments. It will raise their confidence and trust that you will deliver on them.

At the end of a conversation where you've made commitments, summarize your commitments aloud to the other person. If you've written them down, read exactly what you've written aloud to the other person. Afterwards, ask "Did I miss anything?" When you do this, you are making it clear what you are *not* committing to. If the person sees that you are reading what you've written, and you deliver something different from their expectations later, then it's less likely that there will be an I said / you said conversation where someone says "That's not what I agreed to do" or "That's not what I asked you to do. "

Have you ever had a conversation with your boss and found

yourself with an overwhelming list of ten or more tasks? Imagine what would happen if you restated each of those tasks, with delivery dates, to your boss at the end of the meeting, and asked, "Can you help me prioritize which of these ten tasks you would like me to do first?" Often, what you'll find is that other person will start removing tasks from the list for you!

COMMIT TO A FACE-TO-FACE CHECK-IN

If you really want to create accountability for yourself and build trust in the other person that you will live up to your commitments, then proactively suggest a check-in. By agreeing to a face-to-face check in, even if it's just a three-minute video chat, you are agreeing to look the other person in the eyes and tell them what happened. That's much more difficult than sending an email, and it creates an accountability that will skyrocket your probability of delivering on your commitment.

If you are trying to build trust with the other person, or if you think you need the extra accountability, ask them to schedule a time for a check-in when you make the commitment: "Can we schedule a video call or meeting for five minutes on Wednesday at 12 p.m. for a quick face-to-face check-in?"

* * *

As leaders, when we model making commitments in ways that hold us accountable, we set the expectation that everyone on our team makes commitments in a similar way, we reduce drama, and we improve results. What would be the impact on profits, growth, and trust if everyone in your organization made commitments this way?

How much drama and frustration would it eliminate if everyone in your family—and your company—made commitments this way?

* * *

Three years after my first conversation with Mr. Wong, he's still demanding. But now, I've learned how frustrating it is for everyone when commitments are unclear.

Mr. Wong says, "Krister, we require this important feature by next week."

I think, "That's *impossible*! That's six months of work!"

I reply, "Mr. Wong, you will have it on a Wednesday at 5 p.m."

I can hear him taken aback on the phone, and I imagine him smiling with delight at his ability to steamroll me into agreeing to an impossible deadline for the first time in our three-year-long working relationship.

He says, "That's perfect!"

I reply, "Mr. Wong, I said you will have it at 5 p.m. on *a* Wednesday. I did not say *which* Wednesday or which *year*."

It was the first time I heard him laugh.

Actions don't speak. Words do.

Speak your commitments clearly, and action will more likely follow.

Say sorry less.
Apologize more.

*If your relationships haven't improved by
the time you get here, and you've already
said sorry, try apologizing instead.*

I'm riding my bike on the street in Karlsruhe, Germany. I
bump into an older man walking the other way.

"Sorry," I say quickly, unable to remember the German phrase.

I realize that he doesn't speak English. A split-second passes
before I remember the German words for *I'm sorry*.

"*Tut mir leid*," I mumble the German words for *I'm sorry*, but
by now he is far enough away that he didn't hear me.

Isn't that how it goes with apologies? Often our apologies
aren't heard. We use the word *sorry* so often, applying it to

so many situations that, for many of us, it may have lost its impact.

A friend told me about a relationship she had with a man who was constantly "sorry." The word rolled off of his tongue, much like when someone replies "okay" when they want to acknowledge that they heard what you've said but aren't committing much beyond that. I liked the analogy she made: "He uses the word *sorry* like a toll paid that allows him room for misbehavior instead of a fine that brings with it an acknowledgment that he did something wrong."

In other cases, apologies are heard, but not understood because they weren't said using language that the other person understands as an apology.

Gary Chapman is the beloved author of *The 5 Love Languages.* He also wrote about the importance of an apology. I interviewed Dr. Chapman about apologies while researching this book.

Chapman proposes that in order to fully reconcile, an apology needs to be spoken in the apology "language" that is most important to the receiver—not the speaker—of the apology. Often, the person apologizing apologizes in a way that suits their understanding, but their apology isn't heard because the *receiving* person doesn't understand the language of the apology, so to speak.

The words that you say makes a big difference. If you do a word-by-word translation of the German phrase *tut mir leid* into English, it literally translates to *it causes me suffering*. Wow! Imagine how much more powerful your apology would be if it included the words *it causes me suffering*. (The force of the German words makes me wonder if there's a simple linguistic reason why some people are more resistant to apologizing than others.) Sit someone down, look them directly in the eyes, pause for a couple of seconds while looking them in the eyes, and say the following *slowly*:

- I'm sorry.
- I'm deeply sorry.
- I apologize.

Sending a text message or email that says "sorry :)" is not an apology, and don't even think for a moment that it is.

Dropping the words *I am* externalizes your apology and reduces the sincerity and power of your apology. Make sure to include the word *I* as in *I am* sorry or *I apologize*. Enunciate each syllable. Do not use contractions like *I'm*. There is no shortcutting a sincere apology that you want to be received and heard. The words *I am sorry* sound more sincere than *I'm sorry*. For some people, the words *I apologize* are more powerful than *I am sorry* because *I apologize* is an action, whereas *I am sorry* describes a feeling of sorrow. They can effectively be used together as in the above example. Over time in a partnership, you can learn which of these words is more meaningful to your partner because most of us do need to apologize more than once across the span of a partnership.

Look them in the eyes and say it slowly—like you mean it.

If you can't be face-to-face, then use FaceTime or Skype. Eye contact is imperative. It conveys both taking responsibility and commitment.

REPAIRING A BREAK IN THE RELATIONSHIP

Invented in fifteenth-century Japan, *Kintsugi* is an artistic technique for repairing broken pottery using a special lacquer with gold to put the pieces back together. What's fascinating about *Kintsugi* is that the intention is not to disguise the brokenness. The beauty of *Kintsugi* is visibly incorporating brokenness into the new piece.

In *Kintsugi*, the objective is to create a repaired result where the brokenness, while visible, is more beautiful than the original.

Kintsugi is an inspiring metaphor for relationships. Real reconciliation can result in a relationship more beautiful than the original.

A sincere apology can begin the process of reconciliation in a broken or torn relationship.

WHY DON'T WE APOLOGIZE?

Leaders are often the last to apologize. Here is some of what leaders are thinking when they don't apologize:

1. "I am past it. I am focused on the future, not the past."
   Unfortunately, the other person is still stuck in the past.

As a leader, you need to decide whether you will help them get unstuck. You can attempt to convince them of your philosophy, or you can apologize.

2. "But it wasn't my fault. They started it!" If you have more than two kids, you've probably heard this one a lot. Unfortunately, we don't seem to grow out of using this as our reason for failing to apologize. **Put your relationship before your reasons. Apologize.**

3. "My attorney told me it can increase our liability if I apologize." Of course you can discuss it with your legal team, but you also know if you owe the person an apology, so work something out with your legal team that allows for an apology but might not put you at increased risk. Sometimes an apology is all someone needs. In fact, consider the possibility that a sincere apology and a commitment to make things right may be one of the most effective ways to *avoid* a lawsuit.

4. "Apologizing is a sign of weakness" or "If I apologize, then I am acknowledging that I've done something wrong that the person can use against me." Rest assured that they are already holding it against you. The difference is that you're not hearing about it, but likely others are.

WHEN IMPROVING IS NOT ENOUGH

Joe did a 360 survey and his self-ratings were much higher than the ratings of his employees. To his credit, he was courageous enough to call his team together, put the comparison on screen, and ask them directly about it. After much silence, he said, "I think my self-ratings are accurate. You're rating me based upon the leader I was three years ago. Since then,

I've made a lot of changes. I've been to therapy and I've made a lot of effort to improve my communication."

After a long silence, one of his team said meekly, "You know what? I think you're right. But I'm still angry because you never apologized."

If you have improved but your relationship hasn't, consider the possibility that there's a necessary apology that hasn't been said, hasn't been heard, or hasn't been accepted.

THE NON-APOLOGY

Watch for using any phrasing that lets you dodge taking responsibility. This frequently shows up in the words *I'm sorry if* rather than *I'm sorry that*. Saying that you are sorry *if* basically is telling the other person that they interpreted the situation incorrectly rather than you acknowledge that you understand the impact of your actions/words/behavior.

The words that follow *that* are important too. Avoid shirking responsibility by saying something similar to "I'm sorry I upset you" or "I'm sorry you are angry." It's best when your apology is about your own words/actions/behaviors, not their resulting emotions. Also avoid using passive-aggressive phrasing, which is really an expression of your own anger, when you say something like "I'm sorry your mother and I gave you so much that now you are upset that you can't have more."

BUILDING BRIDGES

We advise our friends, or ourselves, "You need to stand up for yourself! Don't let people walk all over you."

In the late 1800s, building bridges was dangerous work. Twenty people died during construction of the Brooklyn Bridge. The Brooklyn Bridge opened in May 1883, after thirteen years of construction.

By definition, a bridge is "a structure that provides people passage over a chasm."

An apology is a bridge of sorts. Apologies pave the way for repairing relationships. What does leadership in partnership look like? Consider that leadership in partnership is taking the lead and being the first to apologize. Sometimes that's taking the lead and apologizing for *your* part in the breakdown in the relationship, even if the other person is not willing to apologize for *their* part.

At the opening celebration of the Brooklyn Bridge, 150,000 people walked across the bridge. P.T. Barnum famously led a parade of twenty-one elephants across the bridge to prove how strong it was.

What if choosing to let someone walk all over you was not a sign of weakness, but a sign of strength—because you are the only one in the relationship who is *strong* enough to be walked on? Sometimes, to recover a relationship, you must build a bridge by *choosing* to allow someone to walk over you to get to a better place. Just make sure your bridge is leading somewhere.

Broken relationships need bridges.

Leaders build bridges.

Be a leader.

Be the bridge.

Conclusion

A confession, an ending, and a new beginning

I have a confession to make. Four years ago, I set out to write an unconventional leadership book for CEOs and senior executives. After rewriting it three times over three years, it became clear that I was really writing a book for leaders struggling with relationships.

Matthew Porter, the CEO with multiple sclerosis who ran a 104-mile ultramarathon, helped me to clarify the vision when he asked me to finish the fill-in-the-blanks phrase that we explored in Talk*SHIFT* #7: The *3 word secret to inspiring people*. I wrote:

If I were ten times more courageous than I am, I would write a series of business books that transform a million marriages, parents, and leaders.

Why does the world need a business book series to bring families together?

Because my (not-so-scientific) research tells me that many successful businesspeople will read 20 business books before they open a single relationship book.

The Talk*SHIFTs* are an effort to meet leaders where they are—in the business section of the bookstore—and expose them to principles of great relationships.

Maybe it's your relationship with your boss or your business partner, your father or your mother, your spouse or your son or your daughter. Maybe it is all of your relationships.

This book transformed my relationship with my father.

I read a previous manuscript to my father—aloud. There were many stories within that were painful for him to hear. It took about six hours to read it to him, and afterwards, he said, "I had no idea how much my words hurt you." While it was a surprise to him that the words of a father to a son would be so harsh, it probably isn't surprising to you. German was my father's native language, and German is a very harsh language. I didn't realize that until I was 45 years old. Unfortunately, my father didn't realize it until he was in his late 70s.

Let me submit the following for your consideration: if your words are unknowingly hurting the people around you—or if the words of someone in your life are hurting you—either you or they will probably want to learn that lesson before you reach your seventies and find yourself looking back on the decades of pain your words have created.

I encourage you to read this book—aloud—to someone in your life. Consider alternating chapters, each of you reading one chapter to the other.

Or, to accelerate your transformation, explore the resources at www.krister.com/support. In addition to many free resources, you'll find the video course, online tools, and immersive transformation weekend events.

You stand at a fork in the road. One path—the well-paved path—leads back to the way you led before. The other path—the path to compassionate leadership—is uncertain, but it leads forward to a new, more peaceful place. Overgrown with weeds, this new path looks less inviting, more challenging.

Which path will you choose?

Will you turn back, or will you forge forward into the jungle of uncertainty?

Like a machete, I hope this book will give you tools to forge forward and cut a path into the jungle that lies before you.

You will stumble. You will fall.

I still do.

As I move on to writing *TalkSHIFTs TWO*, I look back on the content of this book and I see so many mistakes I made that led me to these understandings. I, of course, vow to not make those mistakes again. But I will make mistakes again. They'll just look a little different.

We think we learn our lessons, but in fact, we rarely learn more than 80 percent of the lesson. The remaining 20 percent is there waiting for us—waiting silently, like a parent waiting for a child, or a teacher for a student—the remaining 20 percent sits there patiently, silently waiting for the student to appear once again.

And so we go on—living life's little loop—until we find a true partner who can tell us honestly and compassionately what we look like from their perspective.

That's why we need tools for leadership in partnership. We need tools to guide people on how to compassionately tell us when they see us as we are—and vice versa—without destroying our relationship.

The Talk*SHIFTs* are tools to fuel The Compassion Revolution.

As you consider whether to join The Compassion Revolution, consider this. This is not only *The* Compassion Revolution, it is *Your* Compassion Revolution. For some, The Compassion Revolution will start in the office. But *Your* Compassion Revolution will likely take place closer to home—in your family room, perhaps. *The* Compassion

Revolution may start in a boardroom, but maybe yours belongs in your bedroom.

I don't know where your Compassion Revolution will start, but what I do know is this: every revolution starts with one person asking themselves the same, simple question. Before you start a revolution—or join one—you must answer the question that every revolutionary leader has asked themselves since the beginning of time:

Is this worth fighting for?

But maybe a better question for you is: *who* is worth fighting for?

It's time to shift the conversation. The world needs a Talk-*SHIFT*. *Your* world may need a Talk*SHIFT*.

The journey to mastering the Talk*SHIFT*s is a journey of a thousand suns—and sunsets. Give yourself time. Learning a new language will not come overnight—and neither will a transformation in your relationships.

As you begin your journey, my mind wanders to another French phrase that you probably already know. It rhymes with *bon courage*. We say it to someone before they embark upon a journey...which seems like a fitting way to end our time together.

Bon voyage...

and bon courage, my friend.

Bon courage,

Krister Ungerböck

Krister Ungerböck
Founder of the global TalkSHIFT movement

P.S. I'd love to hear your honest opinion on how this book helped you. Please leave an honest review on Amazon.com. Honest reviews help readers find the right book to fit their needs. Your suggestions will also help us vastly improve the second edition of this book, which will be published in early 2021.

The world needs a Talk*SHIFT*.

Let's spark one.

Together.

Join us.

www.krister.com/join

Raise money for charitable causes when you use your voice, email, or social media to share Talk*SHIFT*s with *your* world. Explore more at www.krister.com/spark.

Acknowledgments

When I first told the publishing pundits that I intended to write a relationship book disguised as a business communication book, they said, "You can't do that!"

And they were right.

As a first-time author, I didn't have the writing skill to do it myself. Writing a relationship book disguised as a leadership book took a powerful pen much more eloquent than my own.

This book is the result of coaching from and collaboration with people who have written over one hundred *New York Times* best-sellers. Over the past four years, it was been written—and rewritten—five times. I often found myself joking, "Why write five books when you can rewrite one book five times?" Three book titles and cover designs. Over six hundred pages written—and four hundred pages deleted.

I am grateful for Nancy Hancock. It was her magic that made

this book magical. If this book transforms millions of leaders, marriages, and families, it was her pen—not mine—that did it. She brought the unique blend of magic this book needed: the fairy-dust magic that makes good great, and the magic-wand magic that transforms goop to gold.

To God, it took a long time for us to reconnect. I now know that you've had a guiding plan for this book. This book would not have been successful even six short months ago. It took far too many fortuitous coincidences—undiscovered trademark issues and repeated delays, culminating in a COVID-19 crescendo—all of these fortuitous coincidences have finally led me to believe that you have a bigger plan for this book, and for each of us. (And thanks to The Crossing Church for being the vehicle that helped me to reconnect with Him again.)

I'm thankful to ten-time *New York Times* best-selling author Neil Strauss, who challenged me to write the book I was born to write. He's much bigger than the man many know as the brilliant marketer and author of the controversial bestseller *The Truth: An Uncomfortable Book about Relationships*. The insights contained in *The Truth* helped me to see my relationship with my mother in a new light, transform my relationship with myself, and let go of the anger toward my father and ex-wife.

To Bob Chapman, CEO of Barry-Wehmiller, and Satya Nadella, CEO of Microsoft, for proving to the world that compassionate leadership also gets business results.

To my father and family members for supporting me and funding this pet project despite our "business divorce."

To the mother of my children and her new husband for exemplifying leadership in partnership as we co-parent our children.

To YPO and EO, the organizations who introduced me to the man who ultimately may have saved my life, and countless other YPO and EO members who made this book possible.

To my mentors and friends, Craig Kirchner, Steve Leclair, Greg Diekemper, and Scott Zimmerman, who read multiple manuscripts and provided detailed, pointed feedback.

To Patience Shutts, for pointing me to the path and providing painstaking feedback on every terrible manuscript that wasn't published.

Thanks to Josh Linkner for encouraging me in a way my father never did.

To Shep Hyken for his patience, toughness, and guidance.

To Brené Brown for writing *Rising Strong*, the book that helped me rise strong.

To my former business partner, Doug Archibald, who taught me compassion and held up a mirror for me to see the leader I wasn't proud to see.

To my CEO coach, Doug Pearson, for asking me the question that changed my life: *Are you inspired by your life?*

To Rusty Shelton, Clint Greenleaf, and the team at Zilker Media for their marketing wizardry.

To Zach Obront at Scribe Writing for his undying patience and truly objective advice. It's hard to find a publishing partner who puts authors' interests above his own!

To Brian Lord and Carl Ware at Premiere Speakers Bureau for taking a chance on me as an undiscovered keynote speaker.

To Chris West at Video Narrative who helped me tell this story in video. His powerful questions helped shape what this book ultimately became.

To my father and family, for supporting me despite our business divorce.

To Tracii, for being my greatest fan and supporting me in more ways than I can write here.

To the hundreds of people who read beta versions of chapters of the book and gave me the feedback that made the book better.

And, finally, to you—for entrusting me with your valuable time.

I hope it was well worth it.

Happiness is a choice.

Let's choose happy.

Resources

By the time you read this, the list below will be woefully out of date. I encourage you to check out the most recent list at www.krister.com/book-resources.

Below is a partial list of the workshops, organizations, and people who inspired my greatest insights—it is their shoulders upon which I stand. If I missed you, please accept my apology. Email me at krister@krister.com and I will make sure your website gets added to the online version and future editions of the book.

Talk*SHIFT* Transformation Weekends. www.krister.com/transformation

Brené Brown. www.brenebrown.com

Chapman and Co. www.ccoleadership.com

Manager Tools Podcast. www.manager-tools.com

The Bell Leadership Institute. www.bellleadership.com

The Compassion Course Online. www.compassioncourse.
org

The Entrepreneurs' Organization. www.eonetwork.org

The Gottman Institute. www.gottman.com

The ManKind Project. www.mankindproject.org

The New York Center for Nonviolent Communication. www.
nycnvc.org

The Strozzi Institute. www.strozziinstitute.com

The Young Presidents' Organization. www.ypo.org

About the Author

KRISTER UNGERBÖCK is a leadership communication expert, keynote speaker, and former CEO of a global tech company. His work has appeared in *NPR*; *Forbes, Inc.*; HR.com; *Chief Executive*; Recruiter.com; and *Entrepreneur*. Prior to exiting corporate life at age 42, Krister was CEO of one of the largest family-owned software companies in the world.

While leading the company to over 3,000% growth, his team won five consecutive Top Workplace Awards, achieved remarkable employee engagement levels of 99.3%, and became a dominant player in its market niche, event-management software.

Bibliography

Brown, Brené. *The Gifts of Imperfection: Let Go of Who You Think You're Supposed to Be and Embrace Who You Are.* Center City, MN: Hazelden Publishing, 2010.

Brown, Brené. *Rising Strong: How the Ability to Reset Transforms the Way We Live, Love, Parent, and Lead.* New York: Random House, 2015.

Chapman, Gary. *The 5 Love Languages: The Secret to Love that Lasts.* Chicago: Northfield Publishing, 2015.

Chapman, Gary, and Jennifer Thomas. *When Sorry Isn't Enough: Making Things Right with Those You Love.* Chicago: Northfield Publishing, 2013.

Fredrickson, Barbara. *Positivity: Top-Notch Research Reveals the 3-to-1 Ratio That Will Change Your Life.* New York: Harmony, 2009.

Gottman, John, and Nan Silver. *The Seven Principles for Making Marriage Work: A Practical Guide from the Country's Foremost Relationship Expert.* New York: Crown, 1999.

Gottman, John, and Nan Silver. *What Makes Love Last?: How to Build Trust and Avoid Betrayal.* New York: Simon & Schuster, 2012.

Rock, David. *Quiet Leadership: Six Steps to Transforming Performance at Work.* New York: Harper Business, 2006.

Rosenberg, Marshall. B. *Nonviolent Communication: A Language of Life: Life-Changing Tools for Healthy Relationships* (3rd ed.). Encinitas, CA: PuddleDancer Press, 2015.

Notes

1   You can watch Bob Chapman's TEDx Talk here: www.krister.com/
truly-human-leadership.

2   I've removed some words to simplify the definition for the purposes of usage
in a business context. The full definition of compassion according to the
Oxford English Dictionary is here: https://www.oed.com/viewdictionaryentry/
Entry/37475.

3   "Pierre-Joseph Proudhon," *Wikiquote*, https://en.wikiquote.org/wiki/
Pierre-Joseph_Proudhon.

4   Harry McCracken, "Satya Nadella Rewrites Microsoft's Code," *Fast
Company*, September 18, 2017, https://www.fastcompany.com/40457458/
satya-nadella-rewrites-microsofts-code.

5   You can find the complete list of needs at the Center for Nonviolent
Communication website at https://www.cnvc.org/training/resource/
needs-inventory.

6   Adapted from the *Manager Tools* podcast episode on delegation: https://www.
manager-tools.com/.

7   Barbara Fredrickson, Positivity: Top-Notch Research Reveals the 3-to-1 Ratio
That Will Change Your Life (New York: Harmony, 2009).

8   You can watch the two-minute viral video *It's Not About The Nail* with your
partner at www.krister.com/the-nail.

9   From "Five whys," *Wikipedia*, https://en.wikipedia.org/wiki/Five_whys.

10   Belinda Luscombe, "How to Stay Married," *Time*, June 2, 2016, https://time.com/4354770/how-to-stay-married/.

11   According to https://kinsta.com/blog/linkedin-statistics, there are 133 million LinkedIn users. According to https://www.statista.com/statistics/269959/employment-in-the-united-states/, there were 155 million employed people in the US in 2018 (133 million divided by 155 million is over 85 percent).

12   "Cognitive dissonance," *Wikipedia*, https://en.wikipedia.org/wiki/Cognitive_dissonance.